W🏋D.BOOK

ATHLETE JOURNAL

CONTENTS

WELCOME

At Wod.Book we devised this athlete journal as the perfect training diary for anyone serious about improving their fitness, tailoring nutrition and tracking goals. We've perfected the book for athletes using CrossFit as a training methodology. While we aren't affiliated with CrossFit, we do advocate the training they provide and as CrossFit Level 1 trainers, Box owners, Military athletes and MSc level researchers, we can confidently say it is the best training regime in the world.

Our book will provide you with everything you need, from movements to programming. So whether you're a member of a box or a lone wolf, you can use our athlete journal for all your workout tracking and advice.

We encourage you to search for the CrossFit Journal on-line and visit CrossFit.com.

STRONG FOUNDATIONS

Getting fit isn't just about high intensity, functional movement and weight loss. Rather, it involves optimising many different aspects of your life to maximise your efforts and support your exercise goals.

GENERAL GUIDELINES

1. Sleeping

Getting enough sleep is absolutely essential for good health, especially when you are engaged in a vigorous exercise regimen. The body uses this time to make repairs, process waste, and carry out general maintenance routines. 8-10 hours per night is ideal.

TIPS FOR GETTING BETTER SLEEP

- Sleep in a pitch black room.
- Avoid caffeinated beverages after lunch.
- Don't sleep with a television or stereo playing. If you must have ambient sounds in order to sleep, try a white noise generator or nature sounds.
- Get outside and active at least 15 minutes each day.
- Eat regular, sensible meals, the last one several hours before bed.
- Avoid sugars such as desserts, wine, and even dried fruit in the evening hours.
- Turn off electronic screens (television, computers, video games) 1-2 hours before bed.

2. Stay Hydrated

Water makes up about 60% of your body's weight. Every system in your body uses water to flush out toxins, carry nutrients to cells, and keep membranes supple. When you don't have enough water, the resulting dehydration can drain your energy and make it more difficult for your body to function. Most people get enough water through the food and beverages they consume, but many things can affect the amount you need, including illness, medications, climate, and activity level. In general, a good rule of thumb is that as long as you rarely feel thirsty, and produce 1.5 litres of colorless or light yellow urine per day, you are probably getting enough water.

TIPS FOR MAXIMIZING WATER INTAKE

- Eat more fruits and vegetables; these can be as much as 90% water.
- Drink before, during, and after exercising. May be in the form of a sports drink, which also replaces sodium lost through sweating.

- Make water your primary beverage choice.

- If you are concerned about your daily fluid intake, your physician or dietician can help determine your requirements.

3. **Regular Meals**

We'll get into specifics on what to eat in the next section, but think proteins, fats, and vegetables. Right now, we're just looking at the general timing and comparative sizes of your meals.

EVERYDAY MEALS

- Breakfast – Eat a large breakfast within an hour of waking. This jump-starts your brain and metabolism, and gives you a strong boost of energy to tackle the day.

- Mid-morning Snack – About a half-meal portion to keep your energy up.

- Lunch – The biggest meal of the day. Try to eat about 4 hours after breakfast. Now you're ready to finish the day!

- Mid-afternoon Snack – About a half-meal portion to get you to the finish line.

- Dinner – This should be the smallest meal of the day, eaten about four hours after lunch and preferably several hours before bed. You don't want to load your body down with more food than it can process before you sleep.

WORKOUT DAY MEALS

All of the above, plus:
- Pre-workout – Protein and fat 30 minutes to 1 hour before your workout.

- Post-workout – Low-fat protein and vegetables dense with carbs within 30 minutes of finishing your workout.

'CHEAT' MEALS

So, you've been good: you've stocked up on healthy food, hit your workout goals, and have gotten plenty of sleep this week. Time to treat yourself! But before you tear into that Cadbury Dairy Milk or Galaxy, consider this:
- 2 slices of Domino's pizza = 600 kcals or 419 burpees

- Pint of Ben and Jerry's Cookie Dough = 980 kcals or 685 burpees.

4. **Proper Nutrition**

Now that you know when to eat, what are you going to eat? And how much per serving? As we mentioned before, when you are planning your menu, you should be thinking primarily about proteins, vegetables, and fats. Look for organic/local versions of all of these in order to avoid refined sugars, pesticides, and preservatives. The portion sizes listed below are general guidelines; your workout regimen may require more of any category at particular times. Your trainer can help you determine your intake requirements based on your goals.

PROTEINS – 1 Serving per meal. 1 Serving = the size of your palm, or a deck of cards.

- Beef (including Bison and Buffalo)
- Chicken and Turkey
- Fish/Shellfish
- Lamb
- Pork
- Eggs/Egg Whites
- etc: sausage and bacon, deli meats, jerky – eat sparingly; check ingredients

VEGETABLES – 1 Serving = As much as you can hold (but take note of the restrictions listed in the key below).

KEY: **Bold** = Nutrient-rich
         Italic = Carb-rich, save for post-workout meals
         <u>Underlined</u> = Glycemic (sugar)-rich, eat at meals earlier in the day, and post-workout

- *<u>Acorn Squash</u>*
- Artichoke
- **Asparagus**
- **Aubergine**
- *<u>Beetroot</u>*
- Beet Greens
- **Bok Choy**
- **Broccoli**
- **Brussels Sprouts**
- *<u>Butternut Squash</u>*
- **Cabbage**
- **Carrots**
- **Cauliflower**
- **Celery**

- Chicory
- **Collards**
- **Cos/Romaine Lettuce**
- **Cucumber**
- **Greens**
- **Kale**
- **Leeks**
- **Mushrooms**
- **Mustard Greens**
- **Onions**
- *<u>Parsnips</u>*
- **Peppers**
- *<u>Pumpkin</u>*
- **Radishes**

- Rhubarb
- **Rocket** (Roquette)
- **Spinach**
- Swede
- *<u>Sweet Potatoes</u>*
- **Swiss Chard**
- <u>Tomatillos</u>
- Tomatoes (yes, yes; technically a fruit, but would you want it in your fruit salad?)
- **Turnips**
- **Turnip Greens**
- **Watercress**
- *<u>Yams</u>*

FATS – 1 or 2 Servings per meal. 1 Serving =
- Oils – coconut for cooking; avocado or olive for salad dressings; approx. 15 ml
- Butter – about a thumb-length
- Green/Black Olives – a full handful
- Coconut (unsweetened) – a full handful
- Coconut Milk (unsweetened) – 1/3 can
- Nuts – fist-sized portion (NO peanuts/peanut butter).
- If high fat loss is a goal, avoid nuts entirely.
- Avocado – ½

FRUITS – 2 servings per day. 1 Serving = a fist-sized portion

KEY: **Bold** = Nutrient-rich

Italic = Carb-rich, save for post-workout meals
NOTE= All fruits are Glycemic (sugar)-rich, eat at meals earlier in the day, and post-workout

Apples	Grapefruit	*Oranges*
Apricots	Guava	**Papaya**
Berries (any)	Honeydew	Peaches
Cantaloupe	*Kiwi*	*Pears*
Cherries	Lemons	*Pineapple*
Dates	Limes	*Plums*
Figs	*Mandarins*	Star Fruit
Grapes	*Nectarines*	Watermelon

BEVERAGES
- Water
- Coffee and Tea (caf or decaf) are both fine, but avoid drinking them near bedtime, and don't add sugar and/or milk.

ETC
- Sauces – check ingredients! No added sugars or dairy.
- Herbs & Spices – go mad with the flavours!

CONVERSION CHART

KILO/LB EQUIVALENTS							
KILOS	LBS		KILOS	LBS		KILOS	LBS
2.3	5		77.0	170		151.6	335
4.5	10		79.2	175		153.9	340
6.8	15		81.5	180		156.2	345
9.1	20		83.7	185		158.4	350
11.3	25		86.0	190		160.7	355
13.6	30		88.3	195		162.9	360
15.9	35		90.5	200		165.2	365
18.1	40		92.8	205		167.5	370
20.4	45		95.1	210		169.7	375
22.6	50		97.3	215		172.0	380
24.9	55		99.6	220		174.3	385
27.2	60		101.8	225		176.5	390
29.4	65		104.1	230		178.8	395
31.7	70		106.4	235		181.0	400
34.0	75		108.6	240		183.3	405
36.2	80		110.9	245		185.6	410
38.5	85		113.2	250		187.8	415
40.7	90		115.4	255		190.1	420
43.0	95		117.7	260		192.4	425
45.3	100		119.9	265		194.6	430
47.5	105		122.2	270		196.9	435
49.8	110		124.5	275		199.1	440
52.1	115		126.7	280		201.4	445
54.3	120		129.0	285		203.7	450
56.6	125		131.3	290		205.9	455
58.8	130		133.5	295		208.2	460
61.1	135		135.8	300		210.5	465
63.4	140		138.0	305		212.7	470
65.6	145		140.3	310		215.0	475
67.9	150		142.6	315		217.2	480
70.2	155		144.8	320		219.5	485
72.4	160		147.1	325		221.8	490
74.7	165		149.4	330		224.0	495
1 kilogram = 2.2046 pounds/1 pound = 0.4535 kilograms						226.3	500

KILOMETRES/MILES							
KM	0.4	0.81	1.2	1.6	4.8	8.1	16.1
MI	0.25	0.5	0.75	1	3	5	10
kilometre = 0.62 miles				mile = 1.6 kilometres			

GLOSSARY

Like any other specialised sport, CrossFit has its own unique lingo. The following glossary defines some of the most common terms and acronyms you'll run across.

AMRAP	As Many Reps/Rounds As Possible
ATG	Arse To Grass
BP	Bench press
BS	Back Squat
BW/BWT	Body Weight
C&J	Clean and Jerk
C2	Concept II rowing machine
CFT	CrossFit Total – consisting of max squat, press, and deadlift.
CFWU	CrossFit Warm-up
CLN	Clean
CTB	Chest To Bar (on Pull ups)
DL	Deadlift
DUB	Double-Unders
FS	Front squat
GHD	Glute/Ham Developer
GHD	Sit up: Sit up done on the GHD bench.
GPP	General Physical Preparedness
GTG	Grease The Groove - doing many sub-maximal sets of an exercise throughout the day
HPC	Hang Power Clean
HSPU	Hand Stand Push Up
HSQ	Hang Squat (clean or snatch)
IF	Intermittent Fasting
KB	Kettlebell
KTE	Knees To Elbows
MetCon	Metabolic Conditioning
MP	Military Press
MU	Muscle-Ups
OHS	Overhead squat
PC	Power Clean
Pd	Pood, weight measure for kettlebells
PJ	Push Jerk
PP	Push Press
PR	Personal Record
PSN	Power Snatch
PU	Pull Ups or Push Ups, depending on context
Rep	Repetition. One performance of an exercise.
RM	Repetition Maximum. Your 1RM is your max lift for one rep. Your 10 RM is the most you can lift 10 times.
Rx'd:	As prescribed; a WOD done without any adjustments
SDHP	Sumo Deadlift High Pull
Set:	A number of repetitions. e.g., 3 sets of 10 reps, often seen as 3x10, means do 10 reps 3 times
SN	Snatch
SPP	Specific Physical Preparedness
SQ	Squat
Subbed	Substituted a specific exercise
TGU	Turkish Get Up
TTB	Toes To Bar
TTD	To The Deck (chest to floor on push ups)
WO	Workout
WOD	Workout Diary

BASIC TRAINING

Master these movements first for safe and effective workouts. Record your maximal efforts and record any coaching feedback points for further improvement.

OVERHEAD SQUAT

Points of Performance

- Feet at shoulder width
- Weight centred on heels
- Head in neitral position
- Chest up
- Bar held over head in wide grip
- Elbows locked
- Knees parallel to feet

Movement Standard

- Knees and hips at full extension
- Hips move back and down
- Maintain lumbar curve
- Bottom of movement is below parallel
- Return to full extension at hips and knees

1 Rep Max					
2 Rep Max					
3 Rep Max					
5 Rep Max					

Coaching Points

FRONT SQUAT

Points of Performance

- Feet at shoulder width
- Weight centred on heels
- Head in neutral position
- Chest upw
- Elbows high
- Arms parallel to ground
- Bar resting on chest
- Hips move back and down

Movement Standard

- Knees and hips at full extension
- Bottom of movement is below parallel
- Return to full extension at hips and knees

1 Rep Max					
2 Rep Max					
3 Rep Max					
5 Rep Max					

Coaching Points

SQUAT SNATCH

Points of Performance

- Feet at shoulder width, slightly turned out
- Hands in wide grip outside of knees; hook grip, arms straight, elbows out
- Shoulders over bar
- Back is flat; chest and head up
- Weight distributed evenly

Movement Standard

- Shoulders and hips rise smoothly
- Knees move back as bar rises
- Quickly shrug the weight with smooth power; hips, ankles and knees reach fulls extension
- Jump under bar to full squat with weight overhead
- Smoothly stand, keeping body tight

1 Rep Max					
2 Rep Max					
3 Rep Max					
5 Rep Max					

Coaching Points

SQUAT CLEAN

Points of Performance

- Feet at shoulder width, slightly turned out
- Hands outside of knees in hook grip
- Shoulders over bar
- Back is flat; chest and head up
- Weight distributed evenly

Movement Standard

- Shoulders and hips rise smoothly
- Knees move back as bar rises
- Quickly shrug the weight with smooth power; hips, ankles and knees reach full extension
- Jump under bar
- Finish in full squat, elbows up, fingers on bar; bar rests on shoulders (above chest)
- Front Squat to stand

1 Rep Max					
2 Rep Max					
3 Rep Max					
5 Rep Max					

Coaching Points

SHOULDER PRESS

Points of Performance

- Bar across shoulders (above chest)
- Hands just outside shoulders, elbows down in front of bar; closed grip
- Feet at hip width

Movement Standard

- Push through heels; keep body rigid
- Bar travels up to locked overhead (pull head back out of bar path; do not tilt chin up)

1 Rep Max					
2 Rep Max					
3 Rep Max					
5 Rep Max					

Coaching Points

POWER CLEAN

Points of Performance

- Feet at shoulder width, slightly turned out
- Weight distributed evenly
- Back flat and tight
- Shoulders over bar
- Head up straight
- Hands outside of knees; hook grip

Movement Standard

- Extend legs; hips and shoulders rise smoothly
- Knees move back as bar rises
- Quickly shrug the weight with smooth power; hips, ankles and knees reach full extension
- Jump under bar and bend knees slightly
- Bar should end resting on shoulders (above chest), elbows up
- Straighten knees

1 Rep Max					
2 Rep Max					
3 Rep Max					
5 Rep Max					

Coaching Points

POWER SNATCH

Points of Performance

- Feet at shoulder width, slightly turned out
- Hands in wide grip outside of knees; hook grip, arms straight, elbows out
- Shoulders over bar
- Back flat and tight
- Head up straight
- Weight distributed evenly

Movement Standard

- Extend legs; hips and shoulders rise smoothly
- Knees move back as bar rises
- Quickly shrug the weight with smooth power; hips, ankles and knees reach full extension
- Jump under the bar and bend knees slightly
- Bar finishes overhead in standing position with arms locked outwards
- Maintain body tension and control as you straighten up

1 Rep Max					
2 Rep Max					
3 Rep Max					
5 Rep Max					

Coaching Points

PUSH JERK

Points of Performance

- Bar across shoulders (above chest)
- Hands just outside shoulders, elbows down in front of bar; closed grip
- Feet at hip width

Movement Standard

- Bend knees slightly and push hips backwards; keep chest straight
- Quickly extend the hip fully
- Press the bar overhead, quickly move body under the bar
- Catch the bar with arms overhead and locked outwards; knees partially bent
- Stand to full extension, keeping bar overhead

1 Rep Max					
2 Rep Max					
3 Rep Max					
5 Rep Max					

Coaching Points

PUSH PRESS

Points of Performance

- Bar across shoulders (above chest)
- Hands just outside shoulders, elbows down in front of bar; closed grip
- Feet at hip width

Movement Standard

- Bend knees slightly and push hips backwards; keep chest straight
- Quickly extend the hip fully
- Press the bar overhead with arms locked

1 Rep Max					
2 Rep Max					
3 Rep Max					
5 Rep Max					

Coaching Points

SPLIT JERK

Points of Performance

- Bar across shoulders (above chest)
- Fingers on bar, elbows slightly down
- Knees straight but not locked
- Feet at shoulder width
- Weight balanced

Movement Standard

- Hips move straight down as knees bend smoothly
- Weight moves from heels to the balls of your feet as you push strongly against the floor
- Jump into split position as weight moves overhead; move hands into hook grip
- Shoulders and hips line up for catch, arms locked
- Move to standing position

1 Rep Max						
2 Rep Max						
3 Rep Max						
5 Rep Max						

Coaching Points

BACK SQUAT

Points of Performance

- Bar across upper back
- Feet at shoulder width
- Weight centred on heels
- Head in neutral position
- Chest up
- Elbows up
- Arms parallel to ground
- Knees parallel to feet

Movement Standard

- Knees and hips at full extension
- Hips move back and down
- Maintain lumbar curve
- Bottom of movement is below parallel
- Return to full extension at hips and knees

1 Rep Max					
2 Rep Max					
3 Rep Max					
5 Rep Max					

Coaching Points

DEAD LIFT

Points of Performance

- Feet between hip and shoulder widths
- Weight centred on heels
- Back arched and slightly slanted upwards
- Shoulders slightly ahead of bar
- Head up straight
- Bar touching shins
- Arms straight

Movement Standard

- Push through heels
- Extend legs: hips and shoulders rise smoothly
- Keep bar against legs
- On return, slightly push shoulders forward and hips back
- Once bar is below knees, steadily bend knees to return bar to floor; maintain proper back angle

1 Rep Max					
2 Rep Max					
3 Rep Max					
5 Rep Max					

Coaching Points

UK HERO WODs

RALPH

British Army Second Lieutenant Ralph Johnson, 24, of South Africa, assigned to the Household Cavalry Regiment, based in Windsor, England, was killed on August 1, 2006, in Helmand province, Afghanistan, when insurgents attacked his vehicle with an improvised explosive device.

For time. Four rounds of:

5 Muscle ups

10 Squat clean

(60k/40k)

20 GHD Sit ups

Date	Time/Reps

HOLKHAM

Dedicated to Daniel Holkham (19) 3rd Battalion The Rifles who died on the 27/03/10 in Afghanistan also dedicated to Lcpl Jonathan Woodgate, Sgt Steven Campbell, Lcpl Scott Hardy, James Grigg Capt Martin Driver, Cpl Stephen Thompson, Lcpl Tom Keogh, Liam Maughan, Jonathan Allott, Cpl Richard Green and Carlos Apolis who in the same month.

2 rounds for time.

25 KB Swing (24/16)

50 Pull Ups

75 Squats

100 Sit Ups

Date	Time/Reps

FOX

Dedicated to Sgt Paul Fox (34) 28 Engineer Regiment who Died in an explosion in Afghanistan on 26/02/10. Also dedicated to Martin Kinggett, Luke Southgate, Lsgt David Walker, Lt Douglas Dalzel Guy Mellors, Sean Dawson, Mark Marshall, Lsgt Dave Greenhalgh, Lcpl Darren Hicks, WO2 David Markland, Cpl John Moore, Seam McDonald, Lcpl Graham Shaw, Cpl Liam Riley.

3 rounds for time.

5 Muscle ups

10 Squat clean

(60k/40k)

20 GHD Sit ups

Date	Time/Reps

AMER

Dedicated to Asgt John Paxton Amer (30) 1st Battalion Coldstream Gaurds, who died in an explosion in Afghanistan on 30/11/09. Also dedicated to Sgt Robert Loghran-Dickson, Cpl Loran Marlton-Thomas, Andrew Fentiman, John Bassett, Phillip Allen, Sgt Phillip Scott, Cpl Nicholas Webster-Smith, Acpl Steven Boote, Sgt Matthew Telford, WO1 Darren Chant.

4 rounds for time.

5 Muscle ups

10 Squat clean

(60k/40k)

20 GHD Sit ups

Date	Time/Reps

COOPER

Dedicated to Lcpl Daniel Cooper (21) 3rd Battalion The Rifles, who died in an explosion in Afghanistan on 24/01/10. Also dedicated to Peter Aldridge, Cpl Lee Brownson, Luke Farmer, Capt Daniel Read, and Robert Hayes who died in the same month.

in a 30 min window, complete:

5 Muscle ups

10 Squat clean

(60k/40k)

20 GHD Sit ups

Date	Time/Reps

RONEY

Police Service of Northern Ireland Constable Ronan Kerr, 25, of Omagh, Northern Ireland, was killed on April 2, 2011 by a car bomb outside his home in Omagh. He is survived by his mother Nuala, brothers Cathair and Aaron, and sister Dainne..

Four rounds of:

Run 200 meters

135 pound Thruster, 11 reps

Run 200 meters

135 pound Push press, 11 reps

Run 200 meters

135 pound Bench press, 11 reps

Date	Time/Reps

MEAD

Dedicated to Nigel Mead (19) Royal Marines Commando, 42 Commando RM (Lima company) who was killed in an Explosion in Afghanistan on 15/05/11 also dedicated to Kevin Fortuna, Ollie Augustin, and Sam Alexander who died in the same month.

20 min AMRAP of:

1 x 15ft rope climb

In pairs, one at a time climb the rope, then out to the carry one partner carry 50m then swap for return 50m.

Date	Time/Reps

MARSHALL

Dedicated to Lcpl Kyle Cleet Marshall (23) 2nd Battalion Parachute Regiment who died in an explosion in Afghanistan on the 14/02/11, and also Robert Wood, Dean Hutchinson, Lewis Hendry, Conrad Lewis, WO2 Colin Beckett and David Dalzell who died in the same month..

For time:

2000m run

Max rep press ups 1min

Max rep sit ups 2 min

Max rep pull ups 1min

Max rep burpees 1 min

300m shuttle sprint (6 x 50m shuttles)

Date	Time/Reps

ADAM

Dedicated to Adam Brown (25) Royal Marines Commando, 40 Commando RM (Alpha Coy) Who was killed in an Expolsion in Afghanistan on 01/08/10.

5 rounds for time of:

7 Chest 2 Bar pull ups

14 Kb swings (32k / 24k)

21 Wall ball (9k / 6k)

Date	Time/Reps

JOSEVA

Dedicated to Joseva Vatubua (24) Argyll and Sutherland Highlanders, who died in an explosion in Afghanistan on the 01/01/11 and also Martin Bell who also died in the same month.

For time:

15-12-9

Bench press

Deadlift

Powerty clean

All performed with bodyweight

Date	Time/Reps

CAPT LISA

Dedicated to Capt Lisa Head (29) Royal Logistics Corps, 11 EODR. Who was killed in an explosion in Afghanistan on 19/04/11.

For time:

1000m run

20 HSPU

20 Toes 2 Bar

20 Pistols

20 Pull ups

20 Burpees

1000m run

Date	Time/Reps

CHARLIE

Dedicated to WO2 Charlie Wood (34) 23rd Pioneers, who died in an explosion in Afghanistan on 28/12/10 also John Howard and Steven Dunn who died the same month..

For time:

100 Burpee pull ups

100 Double unders

Date	Time/Reps

CAMERON

Dedicated to Colour Sgt Alan Cameron (42) 1st Battalion Scots Guards. Who was killed in an explosion on 31/03/11 and also L/Sgt Mark Burgan, Mjr Matthew Collins, Daniel Prior, Lcpl Stephen Mckee and Lcpl Liam Tasker who died in the same month..

For time:

21-15-9

OHS (45k/ 30k) HSPU

GHD Sit up

Date	Time/Reps

CHRISTOPHER

Dedicated to Christopher Davies (22) 1st Battalion Irish Gaurds Who was shot in Afghanistan on the 17/11/10. Also dedicated to Aaron McCormick and Scott Hughes who died on the same month.

For time:

400m run, 21 Thrusters (40k / 20k)

400m run, 21 Pull ups, 400m run

15 SDHP

400m run, 15 Ring dips, 400m run

9 HSPU

400m run

9 OHS,

Date	Time/Reps

BLANCHARD

Dedicated to William Blanchard (39) 101 Engineer Regiment who was shot in Afghanistan on 30/10/10 and also Cpl David Barnsdale, Sgt Peter Rayner, and Suraj Gurung who died in the same month..

15m AMRAP (where one round is)

3 GTOH

3 rounds of

5 pull up

10 press up

15 squat

30 Double unders

Date	Time/Reps

JAMIE

Dedicated to Cpl Jamie Kirkpatrick (32) 101 Engineer Regiment, shot in Afghanistan on 27/06/2010. Stephen Gilbert, Csgt Martyn Horton, Lcpl David Ramsden, Douglas Halliday, Alex Isaac, Sgt Steven Darbyshire RM, Lcpl Micheal Taylor RM, Mne Paul Warren, Mne Richard Hollington, Ashley Smith, Ponipate Tagitaginimoce, Cpl Taniela Rogoiruwai, Mne Steven Birdsall, Lcpl Andrew Breeze, Johnathan Monk, Mark Chandler, Alan Cochran, Cpl Terry Webster, Mne Anthony Hotine.

1000m row

30 Pull ups

30 Thruster (40 / 30)

1000m run

Date	Time/Reps

MATTHEW

Dedicated to Matthew Thomas (24) REME, who died in an explosion In Afghanistan on 25/09/10 and also Cpl Andrew Jones, Andrew Howarth, Darren Deady, Capt Andrew Griffi ths, and Lcpl Joseph Pool who died on the same month..

21- 15-9 of:

Squat snatch (42.5K / 32.5k)

Press ups

Date	Time/Reps

TAYLOR

Dedicated to Marine Scott Taylor (21) 40 Commando RM (Alpha Coy), who died in an explosion in Afghanistan on 30/05/10. Also dedicated to Cpl Stephen Curley RM, Zak Cusack, Cpl Stephen Walker RM, Cpl Christopher Harrison RM, Lcpl Barry Buxton, Daryn Roy, Cpl Alex Holmes who died in the same month.

5 rounds for time:

20 ft rope climb

200m run

20 Press ups

20 Squats

Optional wear a 10k Vest or body armour

Date	Time/Reps

JORDAN

Dedicated to Lcpl Jordan Bancroft (25) Duke of Lancashire Regiment, who was shot in afghanistan on 21/08/10. Also dedicated to Ishwor Gurung, Darren Foster Remand Kulung, Lt John Sanderson Lsgt Dale McCallum and Mne Adam Brown who died in the same month..

For time:

100 KB swings (24k / 16k)

100 Sit ups

100 Squats

100 Push ups

Date	Time/Reps

BURGESS

Dedicated to Jonathan Burgess (23) 1st Battalion The Royal Welsh who was shot in Afghanistan on 07/04/10 also dedicated to Mark Turner and Michael Sweeney who also died in the same month.

30-20-10 of

Pull ups

Burpees

Date	Time/Reps

MARK

Dedicated to Mark Smith (26) 36 Engineer Regiment, who was killed in Afghanistan on 26/07/10. Also dedicated to Lcpl Stephen Monkhouse, Cpl Matthew Stenton, Ssgt Brett Linley, Sgt David Monkhouse, Kinikki Griffi ths, Mne Jonathan Crookes, Lt Neal Turkington, Mne David Hart, Samual Robinson, Thoams Sephton, James Barnett and Cpl Seth Stephens RM who died in the same month.

3 rounds for time:

5 Muscle ups

10 Squat clean (60k / 40k)

20 GHD sit ups

Date	Time/Reps

OLAF

Dedicated to Ssgt Olaf Scmidt (30) 11 EORD, who died in an expolsion in Afghanistan on 31/10/09 Also dedicated to Cpl Thomas Mason, Cpl James Oakland, Lcpl James Hill, Jamie Janes, and Marc Wojtak who died in the same month.

For time:

100 Squat clean thursters (40k / 20k)

Date	Time/Reps

BOLGER

Dedicated to Cpl Stephen Bolger (30) The Parachute Regiment who died in an explosion in Afghanistan on 30/05/09. Also dedicated to Lcpl Nigel Moffett, Lcp Robert Richards RM, Lcpl Kieron Hill, Jordan Rossi, Petero Suesue, Jason Mackie RM, Lt Mark Evison, Adrian Sheldon, Cpl Sean Binnie, Sgt Ben Ross, Cpl Pun Kumar who also died in the same month.

5 rounds of

(with pack or Sandbag 25k)

400m run

25 squats

Date	Time/Reps

NIELD

Dedicated to Cpl Daniel Nield (31) 1st Battalion The Rifl es who died in an explosion in Afghanistan on 30/01/09. Also dedicated to Cpl Richard Robinson, Cpl Danny Winter, Capt Tom Sawyer, Mne Travis Mackin and Sgt Christopher Reed who also died in the same month.

400m run

10 deadlift (110 / 70)

1 rope climb

400m run, 10 deadlift

2 rope climb, 400m run

10 deadlift, 3 ropeclimb, 400m run

10 deadlift, 4 ropeclimb, 400m run

10 deadlift, 5 rope climb

Date	Time/Reps

TOBIE

Dedicated to LSgt Tobie Fasfous (29) 1st Battalion Welsh Gaurds who died in an explosion in Afghanistan on 28/04/09.

400m run, 30 Wall ball

30 Box jump (24 / 20)

followed by 3 rounds of

10 Squat clean (60 / 40k)

10 Press up

30 Box jump

30 Wall ball

400m run

Date	Time/Reps

SEAN

Dedicated to WO2 Sean Upton (35) Royal Artillery who died in an explosion on 27/07/09 in Afghanistan. Also, Lawrence Phillip, Craig Hopson, Christopher King, Capt Daniel Shepard, Cpl Joseph Etchells, Aminiasi Toge, Daniel Simpson, Joseph Murphy, William Aldridge, James Backhouse, Cpl Scott Lee, Cpl Jonathan Home, John Brackpool, Daniel Hume, Christopher Whiteside, Capt Ben Babington-brown, Lcpl Dane Elson, Lcpl David Dennis, Robert Laws, Joshua Hammond and LtCol Rupert Thornloe who died in the same month.

For time:

1000m run

50 Sandbag GTOH (50k / 25k)

1000m run

Date	Time/Reps

BIRCHALL

Dedicated to Major Sean Birchall (33) 1st Battalion Welsh Guards who died in an explosion in Afghanistan on 19/06/09. Also dedicated to Lt Paul Mervis, Robert McClaren, and Cyrus Thatcher who died in the same month.

For time:

100 Back squat (bodyweight)

with 5 Burpees on the minute

every minute until complete

Date	Time/Reps

LASKI

Dedicated to Micheal Laski (21) 45 Commando RM who died in an explosion in Afghanistan on 25/02/09. Also dedicated to Jamie Gunn, Lcpl Paul Upton, Cpl Tom Gaden, Lcpl Stephen Kingscott Mne Darren Smith who also died in the same month.

400m run

50 Burpee pull ups

400m run

50 Burpee pull ups

400m run

Date	Time/Reps

JAMES

Dedicated to Pte James Prosser (21) 34 Squadron RAF Regiment, who died in an explosion in Afghanistan on 27/09/09. Aslo dedicated to Asgt Michael Lockett, Asgt Stuart mcGrath, Brett Hall Jason Dunn-Bridgeman, Cpl John Harrison, Gavin Elliot and Lcpl Richard Brandon who also died in the same month.

For time:

100 Ring dips

100 Ring rows

Partition as required.

Date	Time/Reps

DAVID

Dedicated to David Watson (23) 33 Engineer Regiment, who died in an explosion in Afghanistan on 31/12/09. Also dedicated to Aiden Howell, Lcpl Tommy Brown, Lcpl Christopher Roney, Lcpl Michael Pritchard, Cpl Simon Hornby, James Brown, Lcpl David Kirkness and Lcpl Adam Drane who also died in the same month.

5 rounds for time:

5 Clean & Jerk (60k / 40k)

20 Pull ups

30 Press up

40 Sit ups

50 Squats

Date	Time/Reps

MILLAR

Dedicated to Sgt Stuart Millar (40) The Black Watch, who died in an explosion in Afghanistan on 31/08/09. Also dedicated to Kevin Elliot, Sgt Lee Houltram RM, Shaun Bush, Johnathon Young, Sgt Paul McAleese, Lcpl James Fullarton, Louis Carter, Simon Annis, Sgt Simon Valentine, Richard Hunt, Matthew Hatton, Daniel Wild, Capt Mark Hale, Jason Williams, Cpl Kevin Mulligan Kyle Adams, Lcpl Dale Hopkins and Anthony Lombardi who died in the same month.

3 rounds for time:
Muscle up
14 Thruster (40 / 30)
21 GHD Sit ups

Date	Time/Reps

DEAN

Dedicated to Cpl Dean John (25) REME who died in an explosion in Afghanistan on the 15/03/09. Also dedicated to Cpl Greame Stiff, and Lcpl Christopher Harkett who also died in the same month.

21-15-9 of
Pull ups
Pistols
KB swings (32 / 24)

Date	Time/Reps

ELMS

Dedicated to Cpl Liam Elms (26) 45 Commando RM who died in an explosion in Afghanistan on 31/12/08. Also dedicated to Lcpl Ben Whatley, Cpl Robert Deering, Stuart Nash, Lt Aaron Lewis, Lcpl Steven Fellows, Mne Damian Davies, Sgt John Manual RM, Cpl Marc Birch RM who also died in the same month.

400m run Sandbag or back pack
25kg
then 10 rounds of
10 press ups
10 KB swing (24 / 16)
10 Box jump (24 / 20)
400m SB run

Date	Time/Reps

EVANS

Dedicated to Mne Tony Evans (20) 42 Commando RM who died in an explosion in Afghanistan on 27/11/08. Also dedicated to Mne Georgie Sparks, Mne Alexander Lucas, Csgt Krishnabahadur Dura, Mne Neil Dunstan, Mne Robert McKibben, and Yubraj Rai who all died in the same month.

complete 100 press ups
100 KB swings (24 / 16)
100 T2B
100ft Rope climb (i.e. 10ft climb x 10)

Date	Time/Reps

PETER

Dedicated to Pte Peter Cowton (25) Parachute Regiment 2nd Battalion who died in an explosion in Afghanistan on 29/07/08. Also dedicated to Sgt Jonathan Mathews, Lcpl Kenneth Rowe, and Cpl Jason Barnes who all died in the same month.

3 rounds of:
400m run
21 KB swings (24 / 16)
12 Pull ups
7 min rest
30 GTOH (60 / 40)
400m SB run (25 / 15)

Date	Time/Reps

MUNDAY

Dedicated to James Munday (21) Household Cavalry D squadron who died in an explosion in Afghanistan on 15/10/08.

3 rounds for time of

800m run

20 K2E

30 KB swing (24 / 16)

40 SDHP (40 / 30)

Date	Time/Reps

JOHNSON

Dedicated to Lcpl James Johnson (31) Royal Regiment of Scotland who died in an explosion in Afghanistan on 28/06/08. Also dedicated to WO2 Dan Shirley, Joe Whittaker, WO2 Micheal Williams, Paul Stout, Cpl Sarah Bryant, Cpl Sean Reeve, Lcpl Richard Larkin, Lcpl James Bateman Jeff Doherty, Nathan Cuthbertson, Daniel Gamble, David Murray.

30m AMRAP

5 Deadlift (120 / 90)

7 Pull ups

9 Press ups

Date	Time/Reps

MASON

Dedicated to Lcpl Nicky Mason (26) Parachute Regiment 2nd Battalion who died in an explosion in Afghanistan on 13/09/08, also dedicated to Jason Rawstron, WO2 Gary O'Donnell and Justin Cupples who also died in the same month.

0-5 minutes max rep Squat clean

400m run

10-15 minutes max rep Deadlift

400m run

20-25 minute max rep Squat clean

400m run

Date	Time/Reps

DALE

Dedicated to Mne Dale Gostick (22) Royal Marines Armoured Support Coy, who died in an explosion in Afghanistan on 25/05/08, also dedicated to James Thompson and Ratu Babakubau who also died in the same month.

20m AMRAP

400m run

20ft Rope climb

Date	Time/Reps

DEMPSEY

Dedicated to Cpl Barry Dempsey (29) Royal Highland Fusiliers who died in an explosion in Afghanistan on 18/08/08. Also dedicated to Wayne Bland who also died in the same month.

3 rounds for time of

50 Wall Ball

50 Med ball pressups

50 Ball slams

Date	Time/Reps

ROBERT

Dedicated to Tpr Robert Pearson (22) Queens Royal Lancers who died in an explosion in Afghanistan on 21/04/08. Also dedicated to Graham Livingston and Gary Thompson who died in the same month.

Complete:
10 HSPU
20 GHD sit ups
30 Burpees
40 Pull ups
50 Squats
40 Pull ups
30 Burpees
20 GHD sit ups
10 HSPU

Date	Time/Reps

LT JOHN

Dedicated to Lt John Thornton (22) 40 Commando RM, who died in an explosion in Afghanistan on 30/03/08, also dedicated to Mne David Marsh who died in the same month.

3 rounds for time:
Max rep Clean & Jerk (BW)
400m run
15 GHD sit ups

Date	Time/Reps

GILL

Dedicated to L/Cpl Martin Gill (22) 42 Commando Royal Marines who was shot in Afghanistan on 05/06/11, also dedicated to Martin Lamb, Andrew Found, Lloyd Newell, and Gareth Billingham who died in the same month.

3 round for time
20 toes 2 bar
15 75% bodyweight ground to overhead
3 rope climb
10 burpee box jumps
400m Sand bag run
15 50% bodyweight Over Head Squat
20 pull ups

Date	Time/Reps

MULVIHILL

Dedicated to Cpl Damian Mulvihill (32) Royal Marines, Alpha Coy 40 Commando, who died in an explosion in Afghanistan on 20/02/08. Also dedicated to Cpl Damian Lawrence, and Cpl Darryl Gardiner who died in the same month.

In a 30min window complete:
400m run
10 rounds of
3 HPS
5 OHS
10 OH Lunge
400m run
10 rounds of
3 KB swing (32/24)
5 Burpee
10 Wall ball

in remaining time complete
AMRAP
7 comp press up
7 ring row

Date	Time/Reps

Date	Time/Reps

McLAREN

Dedicated to Scott Mclaren (20) Royal Regiment of Scotland who died in Afghanistan on 04/07/11 Also dedicated to Paul Watkins and Mark Palin who died in the same month.

20min AMRAP

3 50% bodyweight thruster

5 box jump

7 comp press up

Date	Time/Reps

JAMES

Dedicated to James Wright (22) 42 Commando Royal Marines who died on 05/08/11 in Afghanistan Also dedicated to Daniel Clack who died in the same month

In a 20m window accumulate as many points as possible when:

OHS = 10 points

Thruster = 5

Squat clean = 3

Deadlift = 1

All performed with 60k men 40k female

Date	Time/Reps

DAVID F

Dedicated to David Fairbrother (22) 42 Commando Royal Marines who died on 19/09/11, also dedicated to Jonathan Mckinlay who died in the same month.

For time

1000m run 25k sandbag

100 push ups

100 sit ups

100 squats

100 Dbl unders

100ft rope climb (in sets)

1000m run 25k sandbag

Date	Time/Reps

VIJAY

Dedicated to Vijay Rai (21), 2nd battalion The Royal Gurkah Rifl es who died on 15/10/11

For time

50 - 40 - 30 - 20 - 10 of

Burpee pull ups

Sit ups

Date	Time/Reps

LEE RIGBY

Drummer Lee Rigby of the 2nd Battalion the Royal Regiment of Fusiliers was 25 years of age, described as being humorous, generous and loving. "His family meant everything to him, he was a loving son, husband, father, brother and uncle – and a friend to many." He tragically died on the 22nd of May 2013 in an attack close to his home barracks. Drummer Rigby, 25, from Manchester, leaves behind a two-year-old son; Jack, his mother and his step-father and two sisters.

For time:
22 Cal Row
25 Squat Cleans (42.5kg/30kg)
22 Double Unders
25 Bar-hop burpees
22 Double Unders
25 Push Press (42.5kg/30kg)
22 Double Unders
25 Pull Ups
22 Cal Row

Date	Time/Reps

DIESEL
David 'Deisel' Dalzell, a 20-year-old ranger accidentally shot by a comrade as they returned to base from patrol in the Nad-e Ali district of Helmand on 4 February 2011.

1 Clean & Jerk (55k/75k)
300m run
6KB Swings (24k/32k)
20 Burpees

Date	Time/Reps

BAZ
Dedicated to Sgt Barry Weston (40) 42 Commando Royal Marines who died on 30/08/11

Complete as many rounds as possible in 30 minutes of:
30 Double Unders
8 Squat Cleans (70kg/45kg)
11 Hand release Press Ups

Date	Time/Reps

ROYAL MARINES CORPS BIRTHDAY WoD

5 Rounds for time:
28 wall Balls 7/9 kg
10 Squat clean 40/ 60 kg
16 Burpees
64 DU's

Date	Time/Reps

JOHNSON
Dedicated to Sgt Lee Johnson (33) Yorkshire Regiment, who died in an explosion in Afghanistan on 08/12/07. Also dedicated to Tpr Jack Sadler who died in the same month.

30 Box jump (24/20)
3 rounds of
5 hang power clean (all lifts with 40/30k)
10 Push press
15 Back squat
800m run
3 rounds of
5 OHS
10 SDHP
15 Front squat
30 Ball slam
3 rounds of
5 power clean
10 squat clean
15 deadlift

Date	Time/Reps

NOOKIE

Dedicated to Nookie Darnell from Torquay, who died in a Lynx helicopter crash during a search and rescue mission to save the lives of others on 8th December 2004. He was serving on HMS Portland as a Leading Aircraft Mechanic and Winchman. He had already been deployed twice on operations with HMS Portland, and in 1998 he was honoured for bravery with The Boyd Trophy while serving on HMS Iron Duke after saving a life during a search and rescue. Also dedicated to Lt David Cole, 34, Lt Robert Dunn, 29, both from Dorset, Lt Jamie Mitchell, 29, from Dundee who died in the same incident.

20 min AMRAP:
7 x Squat clean 40/30
7 x Push Press 40/30
7 x Back Squat 40/30
200m run (1 lap of HMS Portland)

Date	Time/Reps

facebook.com/britishherowods

@britishherowods

@britishherowods

W🔔D.BOOK

THE GIRLS

ANGIE

For time. Complete all reps before moving to the next exercise.

100 Pull Ups
100 Press Ups
100 Sit Ups
100 Squats

Date	Time/Reps

BARBARA

5 rounds for time Rest 3 minutes between rounds. Add times for each round for total.

20 Pull Ups
30 Press Ups
40 Sit Ups
50 Squats

Date	Time/Reps

CHELSEA

OMEM: On the minute, every minute, for 30 minutes.

5 Pull Ups
10 Press Ups
15 Squats

Date	Time/Reps

CINDY

AMRAP for 20 minutes.

5 Pull Ups
10 Press Ups
15 Squats

Date	Time/Reps

HELEN

3 rounds for time.

Run 400M
21 KB Swings (1.5)
12 Pull Ups

Date	Time/Reps

DIANE

21-15-9

Deadlifts (102/70)
Headstand Press Ups

Date	Time/Reps

ELIZABETH

21-15-9

Cleans (61/43)
Ring Dips

Date	Time/Reps

FRAN

21-15-9

Cleans (61/43)
Ring Dips

Date	Time/Reps

GRACE

For time.

30 Clean & Jerks
(61/43)

Date	Time/Reps

LINDA

10 Reps.

Deadlifts (1.5 BW)
Bench Press (BW)
Cleans (.75 BW)

Date	Time/Reps

ISABEL

For time.

30 Snatches (61/43)

Date	Time/Reps

ISABEL

For time.

Row 1K
50 Thrusters (20/15)
30 Pull Ups

Date	Time/Reps

KAREN

For time.

150 Wall Ball (9/6)

Date	Time/Reps

EVA

5 rounds for time.

Run 800M
30 KB Swings (2)
30 Pull Ups

Date	Time/Reps

KELLY

5 rounds for time.

Run 400M
30 Box Jumps
(61/51cm)
30 Wall Ball (9/6)

Date	Time/Reps

AMANDA

9/7/2005

Muscle Ups
Squat Snatches
(61/43)

Date	Time/Reps

MARY

AMRAP 20 minutes

5 Hanstand Press Ups
10 Pistols/1 Leg Squat
15 Pull Ups

Date	Time/Reps

NANCY

5 rounds for time.

Run 400M
15 OH Squats
(43/30)

Date	Time/Reps

ANNIE

50-40-30-20-10

Double Unders
Sit Ups

Date	Time/Reps

LYNNE

5 rounds for max reps. No time limit.

Bench Press (BW)
Pull Ups

Date	Time/Reps

NICOLE

AMRAP for 20 minutes.

Run 400M
Max Rep Pull Ups
(note # completed)

Date	Time/Reps

US HERO WODs

WILMOT

Six rounds of:
50 Squats
25 Ring dips

Date	Time/Reps

MOON

Seven rounds of:
40 pound dumbbell Hang split snatch, 10 reps Right arm
15 ft Rope Climb, 1 ascent
40 pound dumbbell Hang split snatch, 10 reps Left arm
15 ft Rope Climb, 1 ascent
Alternate feet in the split snatch sets.

Date	Time/Reps

SMALL

Three rounds of:
Row 1000 meters
50 Burpees
50 Box jumps, 24" box
Run 800 meters

Date	Time/Reps

HAMMER

Five rounds of:
135 pound Power clean, 5 reps
135 pound Front squat, 10 reps
135 pound Jerk, 5 reps
20 Pull-ups
Rest 90 seconds between each round

Date	Time/Reps

MOORE

Complete as many rounds in 20 minutes as you can of:
Rope Climb, 1 ascent
Run 400 meters
Max rep Handstand push-up
Score is number handstand push-ups completed for each round

Date	Time/Reps

ZIMMERMAN

Complete as many rounds as possible in 25 minutes of:
11 chest-to-bar pull-ups
2 deadlifts, 315 lb.
10 handstand push-ups

Date	Time/Reps

LOREDO

Six rounds for time of:
24 Squats
24 Push-ups
24 Walking lunge steps
Run 400 meters

Date	Time/Reps

ABBATE

For time:
Run 1 mile
155 pound Clean and jerk, 21 reps
Run 800 meters
155 pound Clean and jerk, 21 reps
Run 1 Mile

Date	Time/Reps

J.J

For time:
185-lb. squat clean, 1 rep
10 parallette handstand push-ups
185-lb. squat clean, 2 reps
9 parallette handstand push-ups
185-lb. squat clean, 3 reps
8 parallette handstand push-ups
185-lb. squat clean, 4 reps
7 parallette handstand push-ups
185-lb. squat clean, 5 reps
6 parallette handstand push-ups
185-lb. squat clean, 6 reps
5 parallette handstand push-ups
185-lb. squat clean, 7 reps
4 parallette handstand push-ups
185-lb. squat clean, 8 reps
3 parallette handstand push-ups
185-lb. squat clean, 9 reps
2 parallette handstand push-ups
185-lb. squat clean, 10 reps
1 parallette handstand push-up

Date	Time/Reps

JT

21-15-9 reps for time:
Handstand push-ups
Ring dips
Push-ups

Date	Time/Reps

MICHAEL

Three rounds for time of:
Run 800 meters
50 back extensions
50 situps

Date	Time/Reps

MURPH

1 mile run
100 pullups
200 pushups
300 squats
1 mile run
*Partition 100-200-300 as needed.
If possible, wear a weighted vest
(V, (insert lbs.))*

Date	Time/Reps

DANIEL

For time:
50 Pull-ups
400 meter run
95 pound Thruster, 21 reps
800 meter run
95 pound Thruster, 21 reps
400 meter run
50 Pull-ups

Date	Time/Reps

JOSH

For time:
95 pound Overhead squat, 21 reps
42 Pull-ups
95 pound Overhead squat, 15 reps
30 Pull-ups
95 pound Overhead squat, 9 reps
18 Pull-ups

Date	Time/Reps

JASON

For time:
100 Squats
5 Muscle-ups
75 Squats
10 Muscle-ups
50 Squats
15 Muscle-ups
25 Squats
20 Muscle-ups

Date	Time/Reps

BADGER

3 rounds for time:

95 pound Squat clean, 30 reps

30 Pull-ups

Run 800 meters

Date	Time/Reps

JOSHIE

3 rounds for time:
40 pound Dumbbell snatch, 21
reps, right arm
21 L Pull-ups
40 pound Dumbbell snatch, 21
reps, left arm
21 L Pull-ups
*The snatches are full squat
snatches*

Date	Time/Reps

NATE

AMRAP, 20 mins
2 Muscle-ups
4 Handstand Push-ups
8 2-Pood Kettlebell swings

Date	Time/Reps

RANDY

For time:
75 lb. Power Snatch, 75 reps

Date	Time/Reps

TOMMY V

For time:
115 pound Thruster, 21 reps
15 ft Rope Climb, 12 ascents
115 pound Thruster, 15 reps
15 ft Rope Climb, 9 ascents
115 pound Thruster, 9 reps
15 ft Rope Climb, 6 ascents

Date	Time/Reps

GRIFF

For time:
Run 800 meters
Run 400 meters backwards
Run 800 meters
Run 400 meters backwards

Date	Time/Reps

RYAN

5 rounds for time:
7 Muscle-ups
21 Burpees
*Each burpee terminates with a
jump one foot above max standing
reach.*

Date	Time/Reps

ERIN

5 rounds for time:
40 pound Dumbbells split clean,
15 reps
21 Pull-ups

Date	Time/Reps

MR.JOSHUA

5 rounds for time:
Run 400 meters
30 Glute-ham sit-ups
250 pound Deadlift, 15 reps

Date	Time/Reps

DT

5 rounds for time:
155 pound Deadlift, 12 reps
155 pound Hang power clean,
9 reps
155 pound Push jerk, 6 reps

Date	Time/Reps

DANNY

AMRAP, 20 mins:
24" box jump, 30 reps
115 pound push press, 20 reps
30 pull-ups

Date	Time/Reps

HANSEN

5 rounds for time:
30 reps, 2 pood Kettlebell swing
30 Burpees
30 Glute-ham sit-ups

Date	Time/Reps

TYLER

5 rounds for time:
7 Muscle-ups
21 reps 95 pound Sumo-deadlift
high-pull

Date	Time/Reps

STEPHEN

30-25-20-15-10-5 rep rounds for
time:
GHD sit-up
Back extension
Knees to elbow
95 pound Stiff legged deadlift

Date	Time/Reps

GARRETT

3 Rounds for time:
75 Squats
25 Ring handstand push-ups
25 L-pull-ups

Date	Time/Reps

WAR FRANK

3 rounds for time:
25 Muscle-ups
100 Squats
35 GHD situps

Date	Time/Reps

McGHEE

AMRAP, 30 mins:
275 pound Deadlift, 5 reps
13 Push-ups
9 Box jumps, 24 inch box

Date	Time/Reps

PAUL

5 rounds for time:
50 Double unders
35 Knees to elbows
185 pound Overhead walk, 20 yards

Date	Time/Reps

JERRY

For time:
Run 1 mile
Row 2K
Run 1 mile

Date	Time/Reps

NUTTS

For time:
10 Handstand push-ups
250 pound Deadlift, 15 reps
25 Box jumps, 30 inch box
50 Pull-ups
100 Wallball shots, 20 pounds, 10'
200 Double-unders
Run 400 meters with a 45lb plate

Date	Time/Reps

ARNIE

For time:
With a single 2 pood kettlebell:
21 Turkish get-ups, Right arm
50 Swings
21 Overhead squats, Left arm
50 Swings
21 Overhead squats, Right arm
50 Swings
21 Turkish get-ups, Left arm

Date	Time/Reps

THE SEVEN

7xFT:
7 Handstand push-ups
135 pound Thruster, 7 reps
7 Knees to elbows
245 pound Deadlift, 7 reps
7 Burpees
7 Kettlebell swings, 2 pood
7 Pull-ups

Date	Time/Reps

RJ

5xFT:
Run 800 meters
15 ft Rope Climb, 5 ascents
50 Push-ups

Date	Time/Reps

LUCE

Wearing a 20 pound vest, 3xFT:
Run 1K
10 Muscle-ups
100 Squats

Date	Time/Reps

JOHNSON

AMRAP in 20mins:
245 pound Deadlift, 9 reps
8 Muscle-ups
155 pound Squat clean, 9 reps

Date	Time/Reps

ROY

5xFT:
225 pound Deadlift, 15 reps
20 Box jumps, 24 inch box
25 Pull-ups

Date	Time/Reps

ADAM BROWN

2xFT:
295 pound Deadlift, 24 reps
24 Box jumps, 24 inch box
24 Wallball shots, 20 pound ball
195 pound Bench press, 24 reps
24 Box jumps, 24 inch box
24 Wallball shots, 20 pound ball
145 pound Clean, 24 reps

Date	Time/Reps

COE

10 Rounds for time:
10 Thrusters @95
10 Ring Pushups

Date	Time/Reps

SEVERIN

50 Strict Pull-ups
100 Push-ups, release hands from
floor at the bottom
Run 5K
If you've got a twenty pound vest
or body armor, wear it.

Date	Time/Reps

HELTON

3xFT:
Run 800 meters
30 reps, 50 pound dumbbell squat cleans
30 Burpees

Date	Time/Reps

JACK

AMRAP in 20mins:
115 pound Push press, 10 reps
10 KB Swings, 1.5 pood
10 Box jumps, 24 inch box

Date	Time/Reps

FORREST

3xFT:
20 L-pull-ups
30 Toes to bar
40 Burpees
Run 800 meters

Date	Time/Reps

BULGER

10xFT:
Run 150 meters
7 Chest to bar pull-ups
135 pound Front squat, 7 reps
7 Handstand push-ups

Date	Time/Reps

BRENTON

5 Rounds for Time:
Bear Crawl 100ft
Standing Broad Jumps 100ft
Every 5 jumps, drop and do 3 burpees

Date	Time/Reps

BLAKE

4xFT:

100 foot Walking lunge with 45lb plate held overhead

30 Box jump, 24 inch box

20 Wallball shots, 20 pound ball

10 Handstand push-ups

Date	Time/Reps

COLIN

6xFT:

Carry 50 pound sandbag 400 meters

115 pound Push press, 12 reps

12 Box jumps, 24 inch box

95 pound Sumo deadlift high-pull, 12 reps

Date	Time/Reps

THOMPSON

10xFT:

15 ft Rope Climb, 1 ascent

95 pound Back squat, 29 reps

135 pound barbells Farmer carry, 10 meters

Begin the rope climbs seated on the floor.

Date	Time/Reps

WHITTEN

5xFT:

22 Kettlebell swings, 2 pood

22 Box jump, 24 inch box

Run 400 meters

22 Burpees

22 Wall ball shots, 20 pound ball

Date	Time/Reps

BULL

2xFT:

200 Double-unders

135 pound Overhead squat, 50 reps

50 Pull-ups

Run 1 mile

Date	Time/Reps

RANKEL

AMRAP in 20mins
225 pound Deadlift, 6 reps
7 Burpee pull-ups
10 Kettlebell swings, 2 pood
Run 200 meters

Date	Time/Reps

HOLBROOK

10 Rounds, each for time of:
115 pound Thruster, 5 reps
10 Pull-ups
100 meter Sprint
Rest 1 minute

Date	Time/Reps

LEDESMA

AMRAP in 20mins
5 Parallette handstand push-ups
10 Toes through rings
20 pound Medicine ball cleans,
15 reps

Date	Time/Reps

WITTMAN

7xFT:
1.5 pood Kettlebell swing, 15 reps
95 pound Power clean, 15 reps
15 Box jumps, 24" box

Date	Time/Reps

WOD.BOOK

WORKOUT RECORD

Date	Mon	Tues	Wed	Thurs	Fri	Sat	Sun
23/03/19				Rate the following for the day: 1-10 (1 is low)			

Nutrition Quality	7	Mood	5
Sleep Quality	4	Recovery	Ok

Summary Crossfit games workout 19.5

33-27-21-15-9 reps for time   PR ✓

30kg thrusters

Jumpin pull ups   — 16.24 mins   Rx ☐

Time cap 20 mins

Date	Mon	Tues	Wed	Thurs	Fri	Sat	Sun
25/03/19				Rate the following for the day: 1-10 (1 is low)			

Nutrition Quality		Mood	Ok
Sleep Quality	Good	Recovery	

Summary

PR ☐

Rx ☐

Date	Mon	Tues	Wed	Thurs	Fri	Sat	Sun
				Rate the following for the day: 1-10 (1 is low)			

Nutrition Quality		Mood	
Sleep Quality		Recovery	

Summary

PR ☐

Rx ☐

Date	Mon	Tues	Wed	Thurs	Fri	Sat	S

Rate the following for the day: 1-10 (1 is low)

Nutrition Quality		Mood	
Sleep Quality		Recovery	

Summary

PR ☐

Rx ☐

Date	Mon	Tues	Wed	Thurs	Fri	Sat	Sun

Rate the following for the day: 1-10 (1 is low)

Nutrition Quality		Mood	
Sleep Quality		Recovery	

Summary

PR ☐

Rx ☐

Date	Mon	Tues	Wed	Thurs	Fri	Sat	Sun

Rate the following for the day: 1-10 (1 is low)

Nutrition Quality		Mood	
Sleep Quality		Recovery	

Summary

PR ☐

Rx ☐

Date	Mon	Tues	Wed	Thurs	Fri	Sat	Sun
	Rate the following for the day: 1-10 (1 is low)						

Nutrition Quality		Mood	
Sleep Quality		Recovery	

Summary

PR ☐

Rx ☐

Date	Mon	Tues	Wed	Thurs	Fri	Sat	Sun
	Rate the following for the day: 1-10 (1 is low)						

Nutrition Quality		Mood	
Sleep Quality		Recovery	

Summary

PR ☐

Rx ☐

Date	Mon	Tues	Wed	Thurs	Fri	Sat	Sun
	Rate the following for the day: 1-10 (1 is low)						

Nutrition Quality		Mood	
Sleep Quality		Recovery	

Summary

PR ☐

Rx ☐

Date	Mon	Tues	Wed	Thurs	Fri	Sat	Sun
	Rate the following for the day: 1-10 (1 is low)						
Nutrition Quality				Mood			
Sleep Quality				Recovery			

Summary

PR ☐

Rx ☐

Date	Mon	Tues	Wed	Thurs	Fri	Sat	Sun
	Rate the following for the day: 1-10 (1 is low)						
Nutrition Quality				Mood			
Sleep Quality				Recovery			

Summary

PR ☐

Rx ☐

Date	Mon	Tues	Wed	Thurs	Fri	Sat	Sun
	Rate the following for the day: 1-10 (1 is low)						
Nutrition Quality				Mood			
Sleep Quality				Recovery			

Summary

PR ☐

Rx ☐

Date	Mon	Tues	Wed	Thurs	Fri	Sat	Sun

Rate the following for the day: 1-10 (1 is low)

Nutrition Quality		Mood	
Sleep Quality		Recovery	

Summary

PR ☐

Rx ☐

Date	Mon	Tues	Wed	Thurs	Fri	Sat	Sun

Rate the following for the day: 1-10 (1 is low)

Nutrition Quality		Mood	
Sleep Quality		Recovery	

Summary

PR ☐

Rx ☐

Date	Mon	Tues	Wed	Thurs	Fri	Sat	Sun

Rate the following for the day: 1-10 (1 is low)

Nutrition Quality		Mood	
Sleep Quality		Recovery	

Summary

PR ☐

Rx ☐

Date	Mon	Tues	Wed	Thurs	Fri	Sat	Sun
	Rate the following for the day: 1-10 (1 is low)						

Nutrition Quality		Mood	
Sleep Quality		Recovery	

Summary

PR ☐

Rx ☐

Date	Mon	Tues	Wed	Thurs	Fri	Sat	Sun
	Rate the following for the day: 1-10 (1 is low)						

Nutrition Quality		Mood	
Sleep Quality		Recovery	

Summary

PR ☐

Rx ☐

Date	Mon	Tues	Wed	Thurs	Fri	Sat	Sun
	Rate the following for the day: 1-10 (1 is low)						

Nutrition Quality		Mood	
Sleep Quality		Recovery	

Summary

PR ☐

Rx ☐

Date	Mon	Tues	Wed	Thurs	Fri	Sat	Sun
	Rate the following for the day: 1-10 (1 is low)						
Nutrition Quality				Mood			
Sleep Quality				Recovery			

Summary

PR ☐

Rx ☐

Date	Mon	Tues	Wed	Thurs	Fri	Sat	Sun
	Rate the following for the day: 1-10 (1 is low)						
Nutrition Quality				Mood			
Sleep Quality				Recovery			

Summary

PR ☐

Rx ☐

Date	Mon	Tues	Wed	Thurs	Fri	Sat	Sun
	Rate the following for the day: 1-10 (1 is low)						
Nutrition Quality				Mood			
Sleep Quality				Recovery			

Summary

PR ☐

Rx ☐

Date	Mon	Tues	Wed	Thurs	Fri	Sat	Sun
	Rate the following for the day: 1-10 (1 is low)						
Nutrition Quality				Mood			
Sleep Quality				Recovery			

Summary

PR ☐

Rx ☐

Date	Mon	Tues	Wed	Thurs	Fri	Sat	Sun
	Rate the following for the day: 1-10 (1 is low)						
Nutrition Quality				Mood			
Sleep Quality				Recovery			

Summary

PR ☐

Rx ☐

Date	Mon	Tues	Wed	Thurs	Fri	Sat	Sun
	Rate the following for the day: 1-10 (1 is low)						
Nutrition Quality				Mood			
Sleep Quality				Recovery			

Summary

PR ☐

Rx ☐

Date	Mon	Tues	Wed	Thurs	Fri	Sat	Sun

Rate the following for the day: 1-10 (1 is low)

Nutrition Quality		Mood	
Sleep Quality		Recovery	

Summary

PR ☐

Rx ☐

Date	Mon	Tues	Wed	Thurs	Fri	Sat	Sun

Rate the following for the day: 1-10 (1 is low)

Nutrition Quality		Mood	
Sleep Quality		Recovery	

Summary

PR ☐

Rx ☐

Date	Mon	Tues	Wed	Thurs	Fri	Sat	Sun

Rate the following for the day: 1-10 (1 is low)

Nutrition Quality		Mood	
Sleep Quality		Recovery	

Summary

PR ☐

Rx ☐

Date	Mon	Tues	Wed	Thurs	Fri	Sat	Sun
	Rate the following for the day: 1-10 (1 is low)						

Nutrition Quality		Mood	
Sleep Quality		Recovery	

Summary

PR ☐

Rx ☐

Date	Mon	Tues	Wed	Thurs	Fri	Sat	Sun
	Rate the following for the day: 1-10 (1 is low)						

Nutrition Quality		Mood	
Sleep Quality		Recovery	

Summary

PR ☐

Rx ☐

Date	Mon	Tues	Wed	Thurs	Fri	Sat	Sun
	Rate the following for the day: 1-10 (1 is low)						

Nutrition Quality		Mood	
Sleep Quality		Recovery	

Summary

PR ☐

Rx ☐

Date	Mon	Tues	Wed	Thurs	Fri	Sat	Sun
	Rate the following for the day: 1-10 (1 is low)						
Nutrition Quality			Mood				
Sleep Quality			Recovery				

Summary

PR ☐

Rx ☐

Date	Mon	Tues	Wed	Thurs	Fri	Sat	Sun
	Rate the following for the day: 1-10 (1 is low)						
Nutrition Quality			Mood				
Sleep Quality			Recovery				

Summary

PR ☐

Rx ☐

Date	Mon	Tues	Wed	Thurs	Fri	Sat	Sun
	Rate the following for the day: 1-10 (1 is low)						
Nutrition Quality			Mood				
Sleep Quality			Recovery				

Summary

PR ☐

Rx ☐

Date	Mon	Tues	Wed	Thurs	Fri	Sat	Sun
	Rate the following for the day: 1-10 (1 is low)						
Nutrition Quality				Mood			
Sleep Quality				Recovery			

Summary

PR ☐

Rx ☐

Date	Mon	Tues	Wed	Thurs	Fri	Sat	Sun
	Rate the following for the day: 1-10 (1 is low)						
Nutrition Quality				Mood			
Sleep Quality				Recovery			

Summary

PR ☐

Rx ☐

Date	Mon	Tues	Wed	Thurs	Fri	Sat	Sun
	Rate the following for the day: 1-10 (1 is low)						
Nutrition Quality				Mood			
Sleep Quality				Recovery			

Summary

PR ☐

Rx ☐

Date	Mon	Tues	Wed	Thurs	Fri	Sat	Sun

Rate the following for the day: 1-10 (1 is low)

Nutrition Quality		Mood	
Sleep Quality		Recovery	

Summary

PR ☐

Rx ☐

Date	Mon	Tues	Wed	Thurs	Fri	Sat	Sun

Rate the following for the day: 1-10 (1 is low)

Nutrition Quality		Mood	
Sleep Quality		Recovery	

Summary

PR ☐

Rx ☐

Date	Mon	Tues	Wed	Thurs	Fri	Sat	Sun

Rate the following for the day: 1-10 (1 is low)

Nutrition Quality		Mood	
Sleep Quality		Recovery	

Summary

PR ☐

Rx ☐

Date	Mon	Tues	Wed	Thurs	Fri	Sat	Sun
	Rate the following for the day: 1-10 (1 is low)						

Nutrition Quality		Mood	
Sleep Quality		Recovery	

Summary

PR ☐

Rx ☐

Date	Mon	Tues	Wed	Thurs	Fri	Sat	Sun
	Rate the following for the day: 1-10 (1 is low)						

Nutrition Quality		Mood	
Sleep Quality		Recovery	

Summary

PR ☐

Rx ☐

Date	Mon	Tues	Wed	Thurs	Fri	Sat	Sun
	Rate the following for the day: 1-10 (1 is low)						

Nutrition Quality		Mood	
Sleep Quality		Recovery	

Summary

PR ☐

Rx ☐

Date	Mon	Tues	Wed	Thurs	Fri	Sat	Sun
	Rate the following for the day: 1-10 (1 is low)						
Nutrition Quality				Mood			
Sleep Quality				Recovery			

Summary

PR ☐

Rx ☐

Date	Mon	Tues	Wed	Thurs	Fri	Sat	Sun
	Rate the following for the day: 1-10 (1 is low)						
Nutrition Quality				Mood			
Sleep Quality				Recovery			

Summary

PR ☐

Rx ☐

Date	Mon	Tues	Wed	Thurs	Fri	Sat	Sun
	Rate the following for the day: 1-10 (1 is low)						
Nutrition Quality				Mood			
Sleep Quality				Recovery			

Summary

PR ☐

Rx ☐

Date	Mon	Tues	Wed	Thurs	Fri	Sat	Sun
	Rate the following for the day: 1-10 (1 is low)						

Nutrition Quality		Mood	
Sleep Quality		Recovery	

Summary

PR ☐

Rx ☐

Date	Mon	Tues	Wed	Thurs	Fri	Sat	Sun
	Rate the following for the day: 1-10 (1 is low)						

Nutrition Quality		Mood	
Sleep Quality		Recovery	

Summary

PR ☐

Rx ☐

Date	Mon	Tues	Wed	Thurs	Fri	Sat	Sun
	Rate the following for the day: 1-10 (1 is low)						

Nutrition Quality		Mood	
Sleep Quality		Recovery	

Summary

PR ☐

Rx ☐

Date	Mon	Tues	Wed	Thurs	Fri	Sat	Sun
	Rate the following for the day: 1-10 (1 is low)						
Nutrition Quality				Mood			
Sleep Quality				Recovery			

Summary

PR ☐

Rx ☐

Date	Mon	Tues	Wed	Thurs	Fri	Sat	Sun
	Rate the following for the day: 1-10 (1 is low)						
Nutrition Quality				Mood			
Sleep Quality				Recovery			

Summary

PR ☐

Rx ☐

Date	Mon	Tues	Wed	Thurs	Fri	Sat	Sun
	Rate the following for the day: 1-10 (1 is low)						
Nutrition Quality				Mood			
Sleep Quality				Recovery			

Summary

PR ☐

Rx ☐

Date	Mon	Tues	Wed	Thurs	Fri	Sat	Sun
	Rate the following for the day: 1-10 (1 is low)						
Nutrition Quality				Mood			
Sleep Quality				Recovery			

Summary

PR ☐

Rx ☐

Date	Mon	Tues	Wed	Thurs	Fri	Sat	Sun
	Rate the following for the day: 1-10 (1 is low)						
Nutrition Quality				Mood			
Sleep Quality				Recovery			

Summary

PR ☐

Rx ☐

Date	Mon	Tues	Wed	Thurs	Fri	Sat	Sun
	Rate the following for the day: 1-10 (1 is low)						
Nutrition Quality				Mood			
Sleep Quality				Recovery			

Summary

PR ☐

Rx ☐

Date	Mon	Tues	Wed	Thurs	Fri	Sat	Sun
	Rate the following for the day: 1-10 (1 is low)						
Nutrition Quality				Mood			
Sleep Quality				Recovery			

Summary

PR ☐

Rx ☐

Date	Mon	Tues	Wed	Thurs	Fri	Sat	Sun
	Rate the following for the day: 1-10 (1 is low)						
Nutrition Quality				Mood			
Sleep Quality				Recovery			

Summary

PR ☐

Rx ☐

Date	Mon	Tues	Wed	Thurs	Fri	Sat	Sun
	Rate the following for the day: 1-10 (1 is low)						
Nutrition Quality				Mood			
Sleep Quality				Recovery			

Summary

PR ☐

Rx ☐

WORKOUT RECORD 75

Date	Mon	Tues	Wed	Thurs	Fri	Sat	Sun
	Rate the following for the day: 1-10 (1 is low)						
Nutrition Quality				Mood			
Sleep Quality				Recovery			

Summary

PR ☐

Rx ☐

Date	Mon	Tues	Wed	Thurs	Fri	Sat	Sun
	Rate the following for the day: 1-10 (1 is low)						
Nutrition Quality				Mood			
Sleep Quality				Recovery			

Summary

PR ☐

Rx ☐

Date	Mon	Tues	Wed	Thurs	Fri	Sat	Sun
	Rate the following for the day: 1-10 (1 is low)						
Nutrition Quality				Mood			
Sleep Quality				Recovery			

Summary

PR ☐

Rx ☐

Date	Mon	Tues	Wed	Thurs	Fri	Sat	Sun
	Rate the following for the day: 1-10 (1 is low)						
Nutrition Quality				Mood			
Sleep Quality				Recovery			

Summary

PR ☐

Rx ☐

Date	Mon	Tues	Wed	Thurs	Fri	Sat	Sun
	Rate the following for the day: 1-10 (1 is low)						
Nutrition Quality				Mood			
Sleep Quality				Recovery			

Summary

PR ☐

Rx ☐

Date	Mon	Tues	Wed	Thurs	Fri	Sat	Sun
	Rate the following for the day: 1-10 (1 is low)						
Nutrition Quality				Mood			
Sleep Quality				Recovery			

Summary

PR ☐

Rx ☐

Date	Mon	Tues	Wed	Thurs	Fri	Sat	Sun
	Rate the following for the day: 1-10 (1 is low)						

Nutrition Quality		Mood	
Sleep Quality		Recovery	

Summary

PR ☐

Rx ☐

Date	Mon	Tues	Wed	Thurs	Fri	Sat	Sun
	Rate the following for the day: 1-10 (1 is low)						

Nutrition Quality		Mood	
Sleep Quality		Recovery	

Summary

PR ☐

Rx ☐

Date	Mon	Tues	Wed	Thurs	Fri	Sat	Sun
	Rate the following for the day: 1-10 (1 is low)						

Nutrition Quality		Mood	
Sleep Quality		Recovery	

Summary

PR ☐

Rx ☐

Date	Mon	Tues	Wed	Thurs	Fri	Sat	Sun

Rate the following for the day: 1-10 (1 is low)

Nutrition Quality		Mood	
Sleep Quality		Recovery	

Summary

PR ☐

Rx ☐

Date	Mon	Tues	Wed	Thurs	Fri	Sat	Sun

Rate the following for the day: 1-10 (1 is low)

Nutrition Quality		Mood	
Sleep Quality		Recovery	

Summary

PR ☐

Rx ☐

Date	Mon	Tues	Wed	Thurs	Fri	Sat	Sun

Rate the following for the day: 1-10 (1 is low)

Nutrition Quality		Mood	
Sleep Quality		Recovery	

Summary

PR ☐

Rx ☐

Date	Mon	Tues	Wed	Thurs	Fri	Sat	Sun
	Rate the following for the day: 1-10 (1 is low)						

Nutrition Quality		Mood	
Sleep Quality		Recovery	

Summary

PR ☐

Rx ☐

Date	Mon	Tues	Wed	Thurs	Fri	Sat	Sun
	Rate the following for the day: 1-10 (1 is low)						

Nutrition Quality		Mood	
Sleep Quality		Recovery	

Summary

PR ☐

Rx ☐

Date	Mon	Tues	Wed	Thurs	Fri	Sat	Sun
	Rate the following for the day: 1-10 (1 is low)						

Nutrition Quality		Mood	
Sleep Quality		Recovery	

Summary

PR ☐

Rx ☐

Date	Mon	Tues	Wed	Thurs	Fri	Sat	Sun

Rate the following for the day: 1-10 (1 is low)

| Nutrition Quality | | Mood | |
| Sleep Quality | | Recovery | |

Summary

PR ☐

Rx ☐

Date	Mon	Tues	Wed	Thurs	Fri	Sat	Sun

Rate the following for the day: 1-10 (1 is low)

| Nutrition Quality | | Mood | |
| Sleep Quality | | Recovery | |

Summary

PR ☐

Rx ☐

Date	Mon	Tues	Wed	Thurs	Fri	Sat	Sun

Rate the following for the day: 1-10 (1 is low)

| Nutrition Quality | | Mood | |
| Sleep Quality | | Recovery | |

Summary

PR ☐

Rx ☐

Date	Mon	Tues	Wed	Thurs	Fri	Sat	Sun
	Rate the following for the day: 1-10 (1 is low)						

| Nutrition Quality | | Mood | |
| Sleep Quality | | Recovery | |

Summary

PR ☐

Rx ☐

Date	Mon	Tues	Wed	Thurs	Fri	Sat	Sun
	Rate the following for the day: 1-10 (1 is low)						

| Nutrition Quality | | Mood | |
| Sleep Quality | | Recovery | |

Summary

PR ☐

Rx ☐

Date	Mon	Tues	Wed	Thurs	Fri	Sat	Sun
	Rate the following for the day: 1-10 (1 is low)						

| Nutrition Quality | | Mood | |
| Sleep Quality | | Recovery | |

Summary

PR ☐

Rx ☐

Date	Mon	Tues	Wed	Thurs	Fri	Sat	Sun
	Rate the following for the day: 1-10 (1 is low)						
Nutrition Quality				Mood			
Sleep Quality				Recovery			

Summary

PR ☐

Rx ☐

Date	Mon	Tues	Wed	Thurs	Fri	Sat	Sun
	Rate the following for the day: 1-10 (1 is low)						
Nutrition Quality				Mood			
Sleep Quality				Recovery			

Summary

PR ☐

Rx ☐

Date	Mon	Tues	Wed	Thurs	Fri	Sat	Sun
	Rate the following for the day: 1-10 (1 is low)						
Nutrition Quality				Mood			
Sleep Quality				Recovery			

Summary

PR ☐

Rx ☐

Date	Mon	Tues	Wed	Thurs	Fri	Sat	Sun
	Rate the following for the day: 1-10 (1 is low)						

Nutrition Quality		Mood	
Sleep Quality		Recovery	

Summary

PR ☐

Rx ☐

Date	Mon	Tues	Wed	Thurs	Fri	Sat	Sun
	Rate the following for the day: 1-10 (1 is low)						

Nutrition Quality		Mood	
Sleep Quality		Recovery	

Summary

PR ☐

Rx ☐

Date	Mon	Tues	Wed	Thurs	Fri	Sat	Sun
	Rate the following for the day: 1-10 (1 is low)						

Nutrition Quality		Mood	
Sleep Quality		Recovery	

Summary

PR ☐

Rx ☐

Date	Mon	Tues	Wed	Thurs	Fri	Sat	Sun

Rate the following for the day: 1-10 (1 is low)

Nutrition Quality		Mood	
Sleep Quality		Recovery	

Summary

PR ☐

Rx ☐

Date	Mon	Tues	Wed	Thurs	Fri	Sat	Sun

Rate the following for the day: 1-10 (1 is low)

Nutrition Quality		Mood	
Sleep Quality		Recovery	

Summary

PR ☐

Rx ☐

Date	Mon	Tues	Wed	Thurs	Fri	Sat	Sun

Rate the following for the day: 1-10 (1 is low)

Nutrition Quality		Mood	
Sleep Quality		Recovery	

Summary

PR ☐

Rx ☐

Date	Mon	Tues	Wed	Thurs	Fri	Sat	Sun
	Rate the following for the day: 1-10 (1 is low)						
Nutrition Quality				Mood			
Sleep Quality				Recovery			

Summary

PR ☐

Rx ☐

Date	Mon	Tues	Wed	Thurs	Fri	Sat	Sun
	Rate the following for the day: 1-10 (1 is low)						
Nutrition Quality				Mood			
Sleep Quality				Recovery			

Summary

PR ☐

Rx ☐

Date	Mon	Tues	Wed	Thurs	Fri	Sat	Sun
	Rate the following for the day: 1-10 (1 is low)						
Nutrition Quality				Mood			
Sleep Quality				Recovery			

Summary

PR ☐

Rx ☐

Date	Mon	Tues	Wed	Thurs	Fri	Sat	Sun
	Rate the following for the day: 1-10 (1 is low)						
Nutrition Quality				Mood			
Sleep Quality				Recovery			

Summary

PR ☐

Rx ☐

Date	Mon	Tues	Wed	Thurs	Fri	Sat	Sun
	Rate the following for the day: 1-10 (1 is low)						
Nutrition Quality				Mood			
Sleep Quality				Recovery			

Summary

PR ☐

Rx ☐

Date	Mon	Tues	Wed	Thurs	Fri	Sat	Sun
	Rate the following for the day: 1-10 (1 is low)						
Nutrition Quality				Mood			
Sleep Quality				Recovery			

Summary

PR ☐

Rx ☐

Date	Mon	Tues	Wed	Thurs	Fri	Sat	Sun
	Rate the following for the day: 1-10 (1 is low)						
Nutrition Quality				Mood			
Sleep Quality				Recovery			

Summary

PR ☐

Rx ☐

Date	Mon	Tues	Wed	Thurs	Fri	Sat	Sun
	Rate the following for the day: 1-10 (1 is low)						
Nutrition Quality				Mood			
Sleep Quality				Recovery			

Summary

PR ☐

Rx ☐

Date	Mon	Tues	Wed	Thurs	Fri	Sat	Sun
	Rate the following for the day: 1-10 (1 is low)						
Nutrition Quality				Mood			
Sleep Quality				Recovery			

Summary

PR ☐

Rx ☐

Date	Mon	Tues	Wed	Thurs	Fri	Sat	Sun
	Rate the following for the day: 1-10 (1 is low)						
Nutrition Quality				Mood			
Sleep Quality				Recovery			

Summary

PR ☐

Rx ☐

Date	Mon	Tues	Wed	Thurs	Fri	Sat	Sun
	Rate the following for the day: 1-10 (1 is low)						
Nutrition Quality				Mood			
Sleep Quality				Recovery			

Summary

PR ☐

Rx ☐

Date	Mon	Tues	Wed	Thurs	Fri	Sat	Sun
	Rate the following for the day: 1-10 (1 is low)						
Nutrition Quality				Mood			
Sleep Quality				Recovery			

Summary

PR ☐

Rx ☐

Date	Mon	Tues	Wed	Thurs	Fri	Sat	Sun
			Rate the following for the day: 1-10 (1 is low)				
Nutrition Quality				Mood			
Sleep Quality				Recovery			

Summary

PR ☐

Rx ☐

Date	Mon	Tues	Wed	Thurs	Fri	Sat	Sun
			Rate the following for the day: 1-10 (1 is low)				
Nutrition Quality				Mood			
Sleep Quality				Recovery			

Summary

PR ☐

Rx ☐

Date	Mon	Tues	Wed	Thurs	Fri	Sat	Sun
			Rate the following for the day: 1-10 (1 is low)				
Nutrition Quality				Mood			
Sleep Quality				Recovery			

Summary

PR ☐

Rx ☐

Date	Mon	Tues	Wed	Thurs	Fri	Sat	Sun
	Rate the following for the day: 1-10 (1 is low)						
Nutrition Quality				Mood			
Sleep Quality				Recovery			

Summary

PR ☐

Rx ☐

Date	Mon	Tues	Wed	Thurs	Fri	Sat	Sun
	Rate the following for the day: 1-10 (1 is low)						
Nutrition Quality				Mood			
Sleep Quality				Recovery			

Summary

PR ☐

Rx ☐

Date	Mon	Tues	Wed	Thurs	Fri	Sat	Sun
	Rate the following for the day: 1-10 (1 is low)						
Nutrition Quality				Mood			
Sleep Quality				Recovery			

Summary

PR ☐

Rx ☐

Date	Mon	Tues	Wed	Thurs	Fri	Sat	Sun
	Rate the following for the day: 1-10 (1 is low)						
Nutrition Quality				Mood			
Sleep Quality				Recovery			

Summary

PR ☐

Rx ☐

Date	Mon	Tues	Wed	Thurs	Fri	Sat	Sun
	Rate the following for the day: 1-10 (1 is low)						
Nutrition Quality				Mood			
Sleep Quality				Recovery			

Summary

PR ☐

Rx ☐

Date	Mon	Tues	Wed	Thurs	Fri	Sat	Sun
	Rate the following for the day: 1-10 (1 is low)						
Nutrition Quality				Mood			
Sleep Quality				Recovery			

Summary

PR ☐

Rx ☐

Date	Mon	Tues	Wed	Thurs	Fri	Sat	Sun

Rate the following for the day: 1-10 (1 is low)

Nutrition Quality		Mood	
Sleep Quality		Recovery	

Summary

PR ☐

Rx ☐

Date	Mon	Tues	Wed	Thurs	Fri	Sat	Sun

Rate the following for the day: 1-10 (1 is low)

Nutrition Quality		Mood	
Sleep Quality		Recovery	

Summary

PR ☐

Rx ☐

Date	Mon	Tues	Wed	Thurs	Fri	Sat	Sun

Rate the following for the day: 1-10 (1 is low)

Nutrition Quality		Mood	
Sleep Quality		Recovery	

Summary

PR ☐

Rx ☐

Date	Mon	Tues	Wed	Thurs	Fri	Sat	Sun
	Rate the following for the day: 1-10 (1 is low)						
Nutrition Quality				Mood			
Sleep Quality				Recovery			

Summary

PR ☐

Rx ☐

Date	Mon	Tues	Wed	Thurs	Fri	Sat	Sun
	Rate the following for the day: 1-10 (1 is low)						
Nutrition Quality				Mood			
Sleep Quality				Recovery			

Summary

PR ☐

Rx ☐

Date	Mon	Tues	Wed	Thurs	Fri	Sat	Sun
	Rate the following for the day: 1-10 (1 is low)						
Nutrition Quality				Mood			
Sleep Quality				Recovery			

Summary

PR ☐

Rx ☐

Date	Mon	Tues	Wed	Thurs	Fri	Sat	Sun
	Rate the following for the day: 1-10 (1 is low)						
Nutrition Quality				Mood			
Sleep Quality				Recovery			

Summary

PR ☐

Rx ☐

Date	Mon	Tues	Wed	Thurs	Fri	Sat	Sun
	Rate the following for the day: 1-10 (1 is low)						
Nutrition Quality				Mood			
Sleep Quality				Recovery			

Summary

PR ☐

Rx ☐

Date	Mon	Tues	Wed	Thurs	Fri	Sat	Sun
	Rate the following for the day: 1-10 (1 is low)						
Nutrition Quality				Mood			
Sleep Quality				Recovery			

Summary

PR ☐

Rx ☐

Date	Mon	Tues	Wed	Thurs	Fri	Sat	Sun
	Rate the following for the day: 1-10 (1 is low)						

Nutrition Quality		Mood	
Sleep Quality		Recovery	

Summary

PR ☐

Rx ☐

Date	Mon	Tues	Wed	Thurs	Fri	Sat	Sun
	Rate the following for the day: 1-10 (1 is low)						

Nutrition Quality		Mood	
Sleep Quality		Recovery	

Summary

PR ☐

Rx ☐

Date	Mon	Tues	Wed	Thurs	Fri	Sat	Sun
	Rate the following for the day: 1-10 (1 is low)						

Nutrition Quality		Mood	
Sleep Quality		Recovery	

Summary

PR ☐

Rx ☐

Date	Mon	Tues	Wed	Thurs	Fri	Sat	Sun
	Rate the following for the day: 1-10 (1 is low)						
Nutrition Quality				Mood			
Sleep Quality				Recovery			

Summary

PR ☐

Rx ☐

Date	Mon	Tues	Wed	Thurs	Fri	Sat	Sun
	Rate the following for the day: 1-10 (1 is low)						
Nutrition Quality				Mood			
Sleep Quality				Recovery			

Summary

PR ☐

Rx ☐

Date	Mon	Tues	Wed	Thurs	Fri	Sat	Sun
	Rate the following for the day: 1-10 (1 is low)						
Nutrition Quality				Mood			
Sleep Quality				Recovery			

Summary

PR ☐

Rx ☐

Date	Mon	Tues	Wed	Thurs	Fri	Sat	Sun
			Rate the following for the day: 1-10 (1 is low)				

Nutrition Quality		Mood	
Sleep Quality		Recovery	

Summary

PR ☐

Rx ☐

Date	Mon	Tues	Wed	Thurs	Fri	Sat	Sun
			Rate the following for the day: 1-10 (1 is low)				

Nutrition Quality		Mood	
Sleep Quality		Recovery	

Summary

PR ☐

Rx ☐

Date	Mon	Tues	Wed	Thurs	Fri	Sat	Sun
			Rate the following for the day: 1-10 (1 is low)				

Nutrition Quality		Mood	
Sleep Quality		Recovery	

Summary

PR ☐

Rx ☐

Date	Mon	Tues	Wed	Thurs	Fri	Sat	Sun
Rate the following for the day: 1-10 (1 is low)							
Nutrition Quality				Mood			
Sleep Quality				Recovery			

Summary

PR ☐

Rx ☐

Date	Mon	Tues	Wed	Thurs	Fri	Sat	Sun
Rate the following for the day: 1-10 (1 is low)							
Nutrition Quality				Mood			
Sleep Quality				Recovery			

Summary

PR ☐

Rx ☐

Date	Mon	Tues	Wed	Thurs	Fri	Sat	Sun
Rate the following for the day: 1-10 (1 is low)							
Nutrition Quality				Mood			
Sleep Quality				Recovery			

Summary

PR ☐

Rx ☐

Date	Mon	Tues	Wed	Thurs	Fri	Sat	Sun
	Rate the following for the day: 1-10 (1 is low)						
Nutrition Quality				Mood			
Sleep Quality				Recovery			

Summary

PR ☐

Rx ☐

Date	Mon	Tues	Wed	Thurs	Fri	Sat	Sun
	Rate the following for the day: 1-10 (1 is low)						
Nutrition Quality				Mood			
Sleep Quality				Recovery			

Summary

PR ☐

Rx ☐

Date	Mon	Tues	Wed	Thurs	Fri	Sat	Sun
	Rate the following for the day: 1-10 (1 is low)						
Nutrition Quality				Mood			
Sleep Quality				Recovery			

Summary

PR ☐

Rx ☐

Date	Mon	Tues	Wed	Thurs	Fri	Sat	Sun
	Rate the following for the day: 1-10 (1 is low)							
Nutrition Quality				Mood			
Sleep Quality				Recovery			

Summary

PR ☐

Rx ☐

Date	Mon	Tues	Wed	Thurs	Fri	Sat	Sun
	Rate the following for the day: 1-10 (1 is low)							
Nutrition Quality				Mood			
Sleep Quality				Recovery			

Summary

PR ☐

Rx ☐

Date	Mon	Tues	Wed	Thurs	Fri	Sat	Sun
	Rate the following for the day: 1-10 (1 is low)							
Nutrition Quality				Mood			
Sleep Quality				Recovery			

Summary

PR ☐

Rx ☐

Date	Mon	Tues	Wed	Thurs	Fri	Sat	Sun
	Rate the following for the day: 1-10 (1 is low)						
Nutrition Quality				Mood			
Sleep Quality				Recovery			

Summary

PR ☐

Rx ☐

Date	Mon	Tues	Wed	Thurs	Fri	Sat	Sun
	Rate the following for the day: 1-10 (1 is low)						
Nutrition Quality				Mood			
Sleep Quality				Recovery			

Summary

PR ☐

Rx ☐

Date	Mon	Tues	Wed	Thurs	Fri	Sat	Sun
	Rate the following for the day: 1-10 (1 is low)						
Nutrition Quality				Mood			
Sleep Quality				Recovery			

Summary

PR ☐

Rx ☐

Date	Mon	Tues	Wed	Thurs	Fri	Sat	Sun
	Rate the following for the day: 1-10 (1 is low)						
Nutrition Quality				Mood			
Sleep Quality				Recovery			

Summary

PR ☐

Rx ☐

Date	Mon	Tues	Wed	Thurs	Fri	Sat	Sun
	Rate the following for the day: 1-10 (1 is low)						
Nutrition Quality				Mood			
Sleep Quality				Recovery			

Summary

PR ☐

Rx ☐

Date	Mon	Tues	Wed	Thurs	Fri	Sat	Sun
	Rate the following for the day: 1-10 (1 is low)						
Nutrition Quality				Mood			
Sleep Quality				Recovery			

Summary

PR ☐

Rx ☐

Date	Mon	Tues	Wed	Thurs	Fri	Sat	Sun

Rate the following for the day: 1-10 (1 is low)

Nutrition Quality		Mood	
Sleep Quality		Recovery	

Summary

PR ☐

Rx ☐

Date	Mon	Tues	Wed	Thurs	Fri	Sat	Sun

Rate the following for the day: 1-10 (1 is low)

Nutrition Quality		Mood	
Sleep Quality		Recovery	

Summary

PR ☐

Rx ☐

Date	Mon	Tues	Wed	Thurs	Fri	Sat	Sun

Rate the following for the day: 1-10 (1 is low)

Nutrition Quality		Mood	
Sleep Quality		Recovery	

Summary

PR ☐

Rx ☐

Date	Mon	Tues	Wed	Thurs	Fri	Sat	Sun

Rate the following for the day: 1-10 (1 is low)

Nutrition Quality		Mood	
Sleep Quality		Recovery	

Summary

PR ☐

Rx ☐

Date	Mon	Tues	Wed	Thurs	Fri	Sat	Sun

Rate the following for the day: 1-10 (1 is low)

Nutrition Quality		Mood	
Sleep Quality		Recovery	

Summary

PR ☐

Rx ☐

Date	Mon	Tues	Wed	Thurs	Fri	Sat	Sun

Rate the following for the day: 1-10 (1 is low)

Nutrition Quality		Mood	
Sleep Quality		Recovery	

Summary

PR ☐

Rx ☐

Date	Mon	Tues	Wed	Thurs	Fri	Sat	Sun
	Rate the following for the day: 1-10 (1 is low)						
Nutrition Quality				Mood			
Sleep Quality				Recovery			

Summary

PR ☐

Rx ☐

Date	Mon	Tues	Wed	Thurs	Fri	Sat	Sun
	Rate the following for the day: 1-10 (1 is low)						
Nutrition Quality				Mood			
Sleep Quality				Recovery			

Summary

PR ☐

Rx ☐

Date	Mon	Tues	Wed	Thurs	Fri	Sat	Sun
	Rate the following for the day: 1-10 (1 is low)						
Nutrition Quality				Mood			
Sleep Quality				Recovery			

Summary

PR ☐

Rx ☐

Date	Mon	Tues	Wed	Thurs	Fri	Sat	Sun
	Rate the following for the day: 1-10 (1 is low)						
Nutrition Quality				Mood			
Sleep Quality				Recovery			

Summary

PR ☐

Rx ☐

Date	Mon	Tues	Wed	Thurs	Fri	Sat	Sun
	Rate the following for the day: 1-10 (1 is low)						
Nutrition Quality				Mood			
Sleep Quality				Recovery			

Summary

PR ☐

Rx ☐

Date	Mon	Tues	Wed	Thurs	Fri	Sat	Sun
	Rate the following for the day: 1-10 (1 is low)						
Nutrition Quality				Mood			
Sleep Quality				Recovery			

Summary

PR ☐

Rx ☐

Date	Mon	Tues	Wed	Thurs	Fri	Sat	Sun
	Rate the following for the day: 1-10 (1 is low)						

Nutrition Quality		Mood	
Sleep Quality		Recovery	

Summary

PR ☐

Rx ☐

Date	Mon	Tues	Wed	Thurs	Fri	Sat	Sun
	Rate the following for the day: 1-10 (1 is low)						

Nutrition Quality		Mood	
Sleep Quality		Recovery	

Summary

PR ☐

Rx ☐

Date	Mon	Tues	Wed	Thurs	Fri	Sat	Sun
	Rate the following for the day: 1-10 (1 is low)						

Nutrition Quality		Mood	
Sleep Quality		Recovery	

Summary

PR ☐

Rx ☐

Date	Mon	Tues	Wed	Thurs	Fri	Sat	Sun
	Rate the following for the day: 1-10 (1 is low)						

Nutrition Quality		Mood	
Sleep Quality		Recovery	

Summary

PR ☐

Rx ☐

Date	Mon	Tues	Wed	Thurs	Fri	Sat	Sun
	Rate the following for the day: 1-10 (1 is low)						

Nutrition Quality		Mood	
Sleep Quality		Recovery	

Summary

PR ☐

Rx ☐

Date	Mon	Tues	Wed	Thurs	Fri	Sat	Sun
	Rate the following for the day: 1-10 (1 is low)						

Nutrition Quality		Mood	
Sleep Quality		Recovery	

Summary

PR ☐

Rx ☐

Date	Mon	Tues	Wed	Thurs	Fri	Sat	Sun
	Rate the following for the day: 1-10 (1 is low)						

Nutrition Quality		Mood	
Sleep Quality		Recovery	

Summary

PR ☐

Rx ☐

Date	Mon	Tues	Wed	Thurs	Fri	Sat	Sun
	Rate the following for the day: 1-10 (1 is low)						

Nutrition Quality		Mood	
Sleep Quality		Recovery	

Summary

PR ☐

Rx ☐

Date	Mon	Tues	Wed	Thurs	Fri	Sat	Sun
	Rate the following for the day: 1-10 (1 is low)						

Nutrition Quality		Mood	
Sleep Quality		Recovery	

Summary

PR ☐

Rx ☐

Date	Mon	Tues	Wed	Thurs	Fri	Sat	Sun

Rate the following for the day: 1-10 (1 is low)

Nutrition Quality		Mood	
Sleep Quality		Recovery	

Summary

PR ☐

Rx ☐

Date	Mon	Tues	Wed	Thurs	Fri	Sat	Sun

Rate the following for the day: 1-10 (1 is low)

Nutrition Quality		Mood	
Sleep Quality		Recovery	

Summary

PR ☐

Rx ☐

Date	Mon	Tues	Wed	Thurs	Fri	Sat	Sun

Rate the following for the day: 1-10 (1 is low)

Nutrition Quality		Mood	
Sleep Quality		Recovery	

Summary

PR ☐

Rx ☐

Date	Mon	Tues	Wed	Thurs	Fri	Sat	Sun
				Rate the following for the day: 1-10 (1 is low)			
Nutrition Quality				Mood			
Sleep Quality				Recovery			

Summary

PR ☐

Rx ☐

Date	Mon	Tues	Wed	Thurs	Fri	Sat	Sun
				Rate the following for the day: 1-10 (1 is low)			
Nutrition Quality				Mood			
Sleep Quality				Recovery			

Summary

PR ☐

Rx ☐

Date	Mon	Tues	Wed	Thurs	Fri	Sat	Sun
				Rate the following for the day: 1-10 (1 is low)			
Nutrition Quality				Mood			
Sleep Quality				Recovery			

Summary

PR ☐

Rx ☐

Date	Mon	Tues	Wed	Thurs	Fri	Sat	Sun
	Rate the following for the day: 1-10 (1 is low)						
Nutrition Quality				Mood			
Sleep Quality				Recovery			

Summary

PR ☐

Rx ☐

Date	Mon	Tues	Wed	Thurs	Fri	Sat	Sun
	Rate the following for the day: 1-10 (1 is low)						
Nutrition Quality				Mood			
Sleep Quality				Recovery			

Summary

PR ☐

Rx ☐

Date	Mon	Tues	Wed	Thurs	Fri	Sat	Sun
	Rate the following for the day: 1-10 (1 is low)						
Nutrition Quality				Mood			
Sleep Quality				Recovery			

Summary

PR ☐

Rx ☐

Date	Mon	Tues	Wed	Thurs	Fri	Sat	Sun
	Rate the following for the day: 1-10 (1 is low)						
Nutrition Quality				Mood			
Sleep Quality				Recovery			

Summary

PR ☐

Rx ☐

Date	Mon	Tues	Wed	Thurs	Fri	Sat	Sun
	Rate the following for the day: 1-10 (1 is low)						
Nutrition Quality				Mood			
Sleep Quality				Recovery			

Summary

PR ☐

Rx ☐

Date	Mon	Tues	Wed	Thurs	Fri	Sat	Sun
	Rate the following for the day: 1-10 (1 is low)						
Nutrition Quality				Mood			
Sleep Quality				Recovery			

Summary

PR ☐

Rx ☐

Date	Mon	Tues	Wed	Thurs	Fri	Sat	Sun
	Rate the following for the day: 1-10 (1 is low)						
Nutrition Quality				Mood			
Sleep Quality				Recovery			

Summary

PR ☐

Rx ☐

Date	Mon	Tues	Wed	Thurs	Fri	Sat	Sun
	Rate the following for the day: 1-10 (1 is low)						
Nutrition Quality				Mood			
Sleep Quality				Recovery			

Summary

PR ☐

Rx ☐

Date	Mon	Tues	Wed	Thurs	Fri	Sat	Sun
	Rate the following for the day: 1-10 (1 is low)						
Nutrition Quality				Mood			
Sleep Quality				Recovery			

Summary

PR ☐

Rx ☐

Date	Mon	Tues	Wed	Thurs	Fri	Sat	Sun

Rate the following for the day: 1-10 (1 is low)

Nutrition Quality		Mood	
Sleep Quality		Recovery	

Summary

PR ☐

Rx ☐

Date	Mon	Tues	Wed	Thurs	Fri	Sat	Sun

Rate the following for the day: 1-10 (1 is low)

Nutrition Quality		Mood	
Sleep Quality		Recovery	

Summary

PR ☐

Rx ☐

Date	Mon	Tues	Wed	Thurs	Fri	Sat	Sun

Rate the following for the day: 1-10 (1 is low)

Nutrition Quality		Mood	
Sleep Quality		Recovery	

Summary

PR ☐

Rx ☐

Date	Mon	Tues	Wed	Thurs	Fri	Sat	Sun
	Rate the following for the day: 1-10 (1 is low)						
Nutrition Quality				Mood			
Sleep Quality				Recovery			

Summary

PR ☐

Rx ☐

Date	Mon	Tues	Wed	Thurs	Fri	Sat	Sun
	Rate the following for the day: 1-10 (1 is low)						
Nutrition Quality				Mood			
Sleep Quality				Recovery			

Summary

PR ☐

Rx ☐

Date	Mon	Tues	Wed	Thurs	Fri	Sat	Sun
	Rate the following for the day: 1-10 (1 is low)						
Nutrition Quality				Mood			
Sleep Quality				Recovery			

Summary

PR ☐

Rx ☐

Date	Mon	Tues	Wed	Thurs	Fri	Sat	Sun

Rate the following for the day: 1-10 (1 is low)

Nutrition Quality		Mood	
Sleep Quality		Recovery	

Summary

PR ☐

Rx ☐

Date	Mon	Tues	Wed	Thurs	Fri	Sat	Sun

Rate the following for the day: 1-10 (1 is low)

Nutrition Quality		Mood	
Sleep Quality		Recovery	

Summary

PR ☐

Rx ☐

Date	Mon	Tues	Wed	Thurs	Fri	Sat	Sun

Rate the following for the day: 1-10 (1 is low)

Nutrition Quality		Mood	
Sleep Quality		Recovery	

Summary

PR ☐

Rx ☐

Date	Mon	Tues	Wed	Thurs	Fri	Sat	Sun
	Rate the following for the day: 1-10 (1 is low)						
Nutrition Quality				Mood			
Sleep Quality				Recovery			

Summary

PR ☐

Rx ☐

Date	Mon	Tues	Wed	Thurs	Fri	Sat	Sun
	Rate the following for the day: 1-10 (1 is low)						
Nutrition Quality				Mood			
Sleep Quality				Recovery			

Summary

PR ☐

Rx ☐

Date	Mon	Tues	Wed	Thurs	Fri	Sat	Sun
	Rate the following for the day: 1-10 (1 is low)						
Nutrition Quality				Mood			
Sleep Quality				Recovery			

Summary

PR ☐

Rx ☐

Date	Mon	Tues	Wed	Thurs	Fri	Sat	Sun
	Rate the following for the day: 1-10 (1 is low)						
Nutrition Quality				Mood			
Sleep Quality				Recovery			

Summary

PR ☐

Rx ☐

Date	Mon	Tues	Wed	Thurs	Fri	Sat	Sun
	Rate the following for the day: 1-10 (1 is low)						
Nutrition Quality				Mood			
Sleep Quality				Recovery			

Summary

PR ☐

Rx ☐

Date	Mon	Tues	Wed	Thurs	Fri	Sat	Sun
	Rate the following for the day: 1-10 (1 is low)						
Nutrition Quality				Mood			
Sleep Quality				Recovery			

Summary

PR ☐

Rx ☐

Date	Mon	Tues	Wed	Thurs	Fri	Sat	Sun
	Rate the following for the day: 1-10 (1 is low)						
Nutrition Quality				Mood			
Sleep Quality				Recovery			

Summary

PR ☐

Rx ☐

Date	Mon	Tues	Wed	Thurs	Fri	Sat	Sun
	Rate the following for the day: 1-10 (1 is low)						
Nutrition Quality				Mood			
Sleep Quality				Recovery			

Summary

PR ☐

Rx ☐

Date	Mon	Tues	Wed	Thurs	Fri	Sat	Sun
	Rate the following for the day: 1-10 (1 is low)						
Nutrition Quality				Mood			
Sleep Quality				Recovery			

Summary

PR ☐

Rx ☐

Printed in Great Britain
by Amazon